PICTOGRAPHICS

ACTUAL DRAWINGS BY
ZACHARY   WISEMAN (AGE SEVEN)

AuthorHouse™
1663 Liberty Drive
Bloomington, IN 47403
www.authorhouse.com
Phone: 1-800-839-8640

First published by AuthorHouse   6/18/2010

ISBN: 978-1-4490-8715-9 (e)
ISBN: 978-1-4490-8714-2 (sc)

Library of Congress Control Number: 2010908520

Printed in the United States of America
Bloomington, Indiana

This book is printed on acid-free paper.

Other books by this author

"The Nature of Centered Emotion"

"Become as a Child"

CONTENTS

INTRODUCTION

INTRODUCTION

"Art is a form of supremely delicate awareness...meaning at-oneness, the state of being at one with the object... The picture must all come out of the artist's inside... It is the image that lives in the consciousness, alive like a vision, but unknown."

D.H. Lawrence

This quote by D.H. Lawrence best sums up the very young child's state of mind as he or she draws. Unformed mental images, below the surface of conscious awareness, take form on paper, becoming real before his or her eyes.

THE EARLY DRAWINGS

The young child's drawings reflect a balance, wholeness and pureness of style reflecting honesty and innocence of perception. During this stage of drawing, at approximate ages of 5 to 8 years, the child is not concerned with reproducing exact likenesses of what he sees outwardly but what he sees in his mind's eye, which is his own creation of reality. It is this very special age group, and these drawings, this book focuses on.

The older child's perception shifts from this inner mental creativity, which appears to be a vital part of mental development, to focusing on the exterior world. At this stage most older children turn to drawing cartoon likenesses of their favorite objects such as comic book heroes, fantasy automobiles and drawings reflecting the concerns of pre-teen age boys and girls. *This type of symbolic drawing reflects conscious desires and is not representative of the spontaneous introspective drawing of the younger child.*

Spontaneous drawing is one of the joys of childhood. The fact is, this simple pleasure is left behind all too soon; so brief is it's time. A time when you could get lost in the miracle of making things appear where before there was nothing. When you and the blank piece of paper and the pencil formed a trinity opening up new worlds into the wonders of self expression.

What educators see as a stepping stone to greater artistic abilities is actually an arrival, a special time with a special purpose of it's own. Spontaneous drawings have depth beyond that of dimensional perspective as seen by the eye. This depth reaches into and beyond the actual forms as they appear to the casual viewer. These drawings are expressions of the unconscious. The ability to pour forth these images, placing, ordering and pouring unformed feelings into a drawing that expresses exactly how he or she feels, comes naturally to the child.

This book explores this idea and presents a method for more clearly understanding the psychological implications of object placement in these early childhood drawings and to use this information to open new lines of communication between child and adult.

THE CHILD'S GRAPHIC TOOLS

THE CIRCLE-SQUARE-DIAMOND-OVAL-RECTANGLE AND THE GREEK AND DIAGONAL CROSSES

This book will show you how the child spontaneously uses these seven geometric forms as graphic tools; forming wholes, segments and combines to construct and symbolize familiar objects. Familiar objects convey their own symbolic meanings which are commonly accepted by everyone. The house is symbolic of home and family, the stick figure can be anyone the child wishes it to be; self, mother, father, teacher, etc. You are already familiar with these types of symbolic drawings and no doubt drew them yourself as a child.

PICTOGRAPHICS REVEALS THE PSYCHOLOGICAL IMPLICATIONS OF PLACEMENT OF THESE FAMILIAR OBJECTS ON THE DRAWING PAPER.

THE CROSSED CIRCLE

The crossed circle is a favorite drawing among young children. This is one version of a Mandala - a circle crossed with lines. This Mandala appears in many historical works of art. As this same crossed circle appears universally in works of art it seems that an innate awareness of this formation is common to all people.

The renowned psychoanalyst, Carl Jung, (Man and His Symbols), was an enthusiastic student of the Mandala. This interest highly influenced his later years as a psychoanalyst. After a personal experience, in which he conceived of and painted Mandalas, he believed them to be symbols acting as mediators between the conscious and the unconscious. It was his belief that the drawing of these forms indicate a personally conceived awareness of a universal human experience. The construct of Mandalas can range from the simple circle to complex ornate constructions. For a more detailed understanding of the Mandala and its origins, a book titled *Mandala* by Jose and Miriam Arguelles is available from Shambhala Publishing.

PICTOGRAPHICS GRID AND SYMBOL SYSTEM

This system is based on the simplest of formats suggested by the "rays" of the symbol of the sun when placed at the center of the drawing paper. Radiating outwardly, from a circular center, they point to familiar physical orientations; Up-down/ In-Out. The diagonal "rays" divide the drawing paper into four areas representative of these orientations.

Beginning with the circle as the Center the seven basic geometrical forms, as used in the Pictographic symbol system, result in a symbolic self association with the Center of the drawing paper. By observing the placement of familiar objects, compared to the Center of the drawing, the artist's subconscious emotional orientations are revealed. This *psychological* orientation is compatible with the physical orientations of the drawing paper. Up-Down refers to feeling Up as opposed to feeling Down. Out-In relates to common references of an Outer and as opposed to an Inner sense of self.

The basic placement interpretations shown in this book are comparable to those recognized by many professionals interested in the psychological implications of children's drawings. *Every* placement interpretation evolved from, and inter-relates with, the basic Up-Down/In-Out patterning. What is different about this book is the underlying format that brings these placement ideas together in a unified whole; making it possible for the average parent to apply these principles to their children's drawings.

As physical and psychological orientations evolve on a grid that is transferable to any size paper, it becomes an accurate guide to the further understanding of any spontaneous drawing. A step by step guided tour of the drawing field will familiarize you with the grid and symbol system presented in this book. In the form of a text book, it is not meant for random reading. Because each step is dependent upon the one before it, It is important that you read each section in the progressive order it is presented.

VISUAL
CENTERING

GUIDE TO DRAWING PAPER ORIENTATION

 1

VISUAL CENTERING

The eye movements of the infant, as observed by child development specialists, suggest a visual/mental centering. As the infant turns his head, from one direction to another, the movement of the eyes "structure" the new field of vision by quickly moving up-down, right-left and diagonally. These eye movements indicate that a mental structuring of a viewing field coincides with the visual orientation processes. This fixed field of vision "frames" and organizes whatever scene the eyes are focused on.

DRAWING FIELD ORIENTATIONS DEFINED BY LINES OF THE CROSSED CIRCLE:

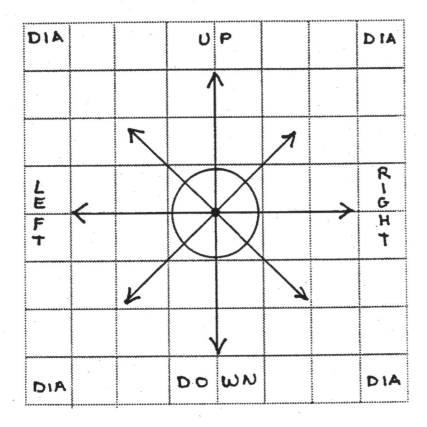

The lines of the Crossed Circle, placed at the center of the drawing paper, relate to the orientations defined by the hypothetical viewing field. The viewing field organizes an existing scene, while the blank drawing paper presents the artist with an orientationally organized "drawing field" upon which to project his inner mental visions.

To a child it seems that every part of the drawing surface has symbolic meaning, the empty spaces surface functioning as air through which smoke rises, the sun's rays shine, and birds fly.

-Betty Edwards
Drawing On the Right Side of the Brain

GUIDED TOUR

OF THE DRAWING FIELD

 2

OUTER EDGES OF THE DRAWING FIELD :

TOP- BOTTOM   *   LEFT-RIGHT

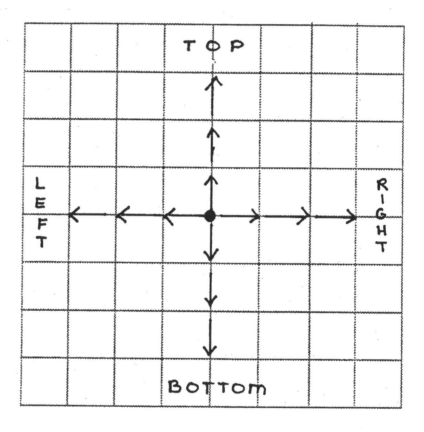

THE VERTICAL LINE POINTS TO THE TOP AND BOTTOM EDGES

THE HORIZONTAL LINE POINTS TO THE LEFT AND RIGHT EDGES

DIAGONAL LINES CREATE AREA BOUNDARIES WITHIN DRAWING FIELD:

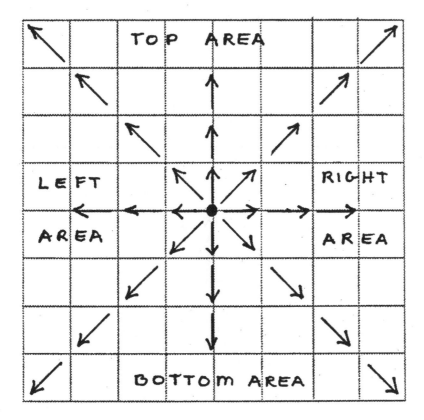

DIAGONAL LINES ACT AS BOUNDARY LINES CREATING FOUR OPPOSITIONALLY BASED AREAS ON THE DRAWING FIELD.

These diagonal visual orientations might normally go unnoticed as they are not consciously noted in normal horizontal/vertical vision. In Pictographics, these diagonal lines initially serve to divide the drawing field into *areas* common to the top-bottom and left-right edges of the paper.

THE TOP-BOTTOM VERTICAL LINE ESTABLISHES AN UP-DOWN

VERTICAL *FOCUS* OF THE DRAWING FIELD:

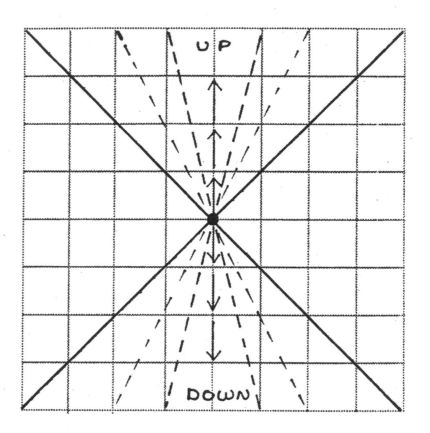

As the sky is Up; Clouds, kites, suns, birds, etc. are placed up at the TOP of the paper.   The ground is down, so Grass, trees, ground lines, etc. are placed down at the BOTTOM of the paper.

READING FROM THE CENTER HORIZONTALLY:

THE *FOCUS* TO THE LEFT LOOKS IN AND THE *FOCUS* TO THE RIGHT LOOKS OUT

This center oriented, left to right focus has been observed existing in certain examples of ancient Egyptian hieroglyphics; the symbols faced the center, so that one read from the center outwardly in both directions:

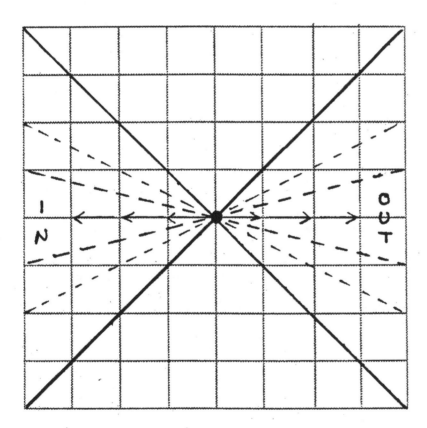

Most handwriting, in the Western world, moves from left to right. This promotes the feeling of "moving outwards" toward the right. Logically then, moving toward the left is to "move inwards". The Center perspective establishes a point of reference between the two directions.

FOUR OPPOSITIONAL AREAS OF FOCUS:

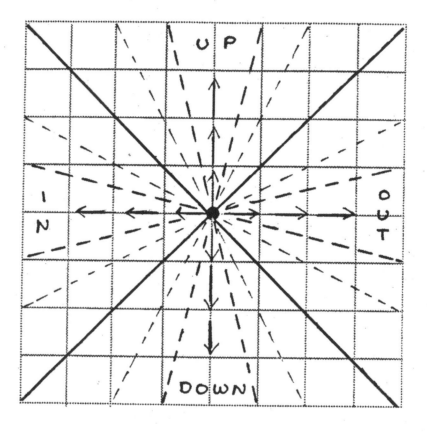

VERTICAL *FOCUS*   AREAS: UP-DOWN

HORIZONTAL *FOCUS*   AREAS: IN-OUT

Two sets of opposites, define four Areas of focus.   Up vs. Down and In vs. Out. These four Areas, surrounding a Centered Perspective, establish a physically oriented drawing field concept.

CENTERED   PERSPECTIVE   GRID:

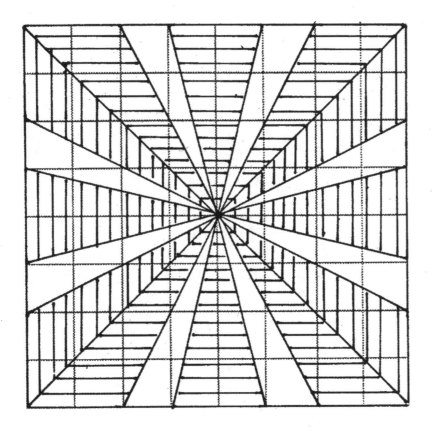

With the addition of secondary vertical and horizontal lines connecting the Area focus lines, this graph takes on a more recognizable version of what is typically referred to as *perspective* in relation to drawing. When all lines converge at the center of a drawing, it is   called the center vanishing point.   As used in Pictographics this center vanishing point establishes a *Central Focus*   to which all objects are relative.

COMPARED TO THE PERSPECTIVE ESTABLISHED BY
THE *CENTER VANISHING POINT* THE FOLLOWING DRAWING
APPEARS TO BE FLAT AND WITHOUT DEPTH:

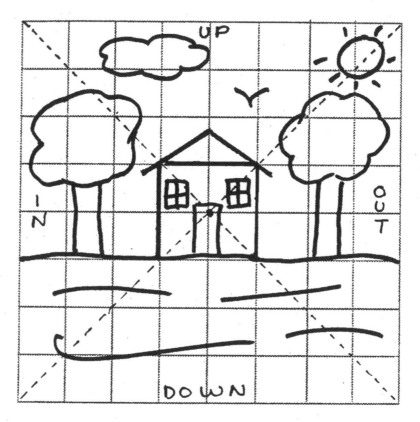

SHARING THE CHILD'S PERSPECTIVE

By applying Pictographic's Four Area Focus to these drawings
you will begin to see beyond the surface and into another kind
of orientation, one where all objects in the drawing are
relative to the *center* of the drawing field and the perspective
is psychological as well as physical.

PSYCHOLOGICAL
ASSOCIATIONS

WITH THE DRAWING FIELD

 3

DOODLES

The first three basic forms used in this book are commonly recognized "doodles". Modern psychology has long recognized the psychological implications of these innocent appearing scribbles and their use in helping to understand human behavior. While the particular execution of a doodle is unique to each individual certain forms are generally accepted to indicate particular meanings.

Although this book is not meant for the interpretation of doodles, as such, the following generally accepted symbolic meanings of the Circle, Square and Diamond are applied to the grid in order to provide a sense of centered orientation on the drawing field.

THE PSYCHOLOGY OF THE CIRCLE:

The Wartegg drawing test, developed and widely used in Europe for assessing personality, assumes a dot centered on a page is an unconscious symbol representing self or ego. This central positioning indicates aspects of the artists emotional response to his surroundings.

BASIC FORM NUMBER ONE: THE CIRCLE

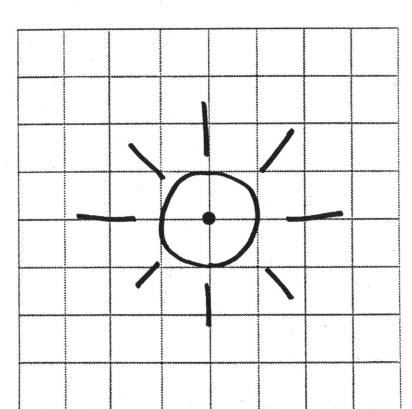

Here, the centered dot expands becoming the circle. The circle has been recognized as a symbol of self essence since prehistoric man carved suns on the walls of their cave dwellings. Circles are symbols of the essence of things. When a child draws the sun, he is drawing a picture of the life, light and warmth he feels himself to be. This energy is expressed as the *rays* of the sun.

BASIC FORM NUMBER TWO: THE SQUARE

As the Circle indicates ego sensitivity on the part of the artist, the Square is another aspect of that same self awareness;   representing a more practical frame of mind. The Square is a symbol of self security.

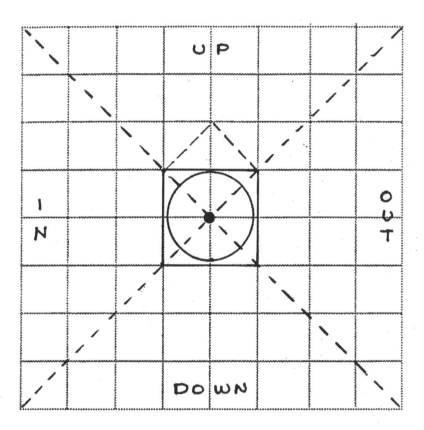

This example shows the Square, constructing the outlines of a house. As the Square is a symbol of *security* so is the house.

According to prominent graphologists the most common placement of a primary object drawn on a page is the center. (It has been suggested that a person who draws **"only"** centered objects may be timid and unadventurous). However, this central placement generally reflects the feelings of the normal well grounded, confident person.

BASIC FORM NUMBER THREE: THE DIAMOND

Angles and Arrows in a drawing are generally accepted as signs of aggression and determination. The Diamond symbol forms four arrows, each pointing to an Area of the drawing field:

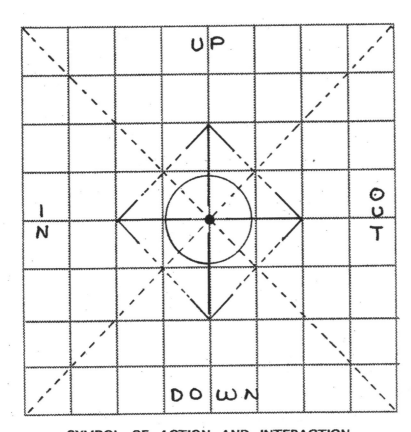

SYMBOL OF ACTION AND INTERACTION

In Pictographics, the four arrow Diamond becomes a symbol of action, interaction, and reaction. Here, the Diamond is a symbol of self in action where feelings of aggression, determination, or other feelings may also be indicated by the placement of particular objects in one of the Areas.

CENTERED SELF PERSPECTIVE

Self identification and feelings of security are psychologically associated with the center of the drawing field. To feel *centered* is to feel emotionally balanced between the constant fluctuation of opposing feelings. The Diamond is a related *action* symbol allowing for the expression of varying feelings in different areas of the drawing field.

The closely knit relationships of these three forms can be viewed by doing the following exercise: Cut a cardboard square of approximately two inches. Fasten it loosely at the center with a pin to a firm foundation. Spin the square with the tip of your finger to set it in motion. You will see that at high speed the square appears to be a Circle. As it slows down a Diamond shape is visible, before it stops, becoming a Square again.

PHYSICAL AND PSYCHOLOGICAL ASSOCIATIONS WITH THE DRAWING FIELD

Physical and psychological associations with the drawing field are closely related. Words used to describe emotions are in many cases the same words we use to describe directions. When we are depressed, we say we feel "down". Feeling "up" is interchangeable with feeling happy. These particular associations conform with the vertical UP-DOWN focus of the drawing field.

Coming in and going out physically apply to arriving and leaving a given place. Psychologically, these references are used to refer to an **inner** private sense of self as opposed to a more public **outer** picture of self.

INNER - OUTER AREAS
HORIZONTAL FOCUS

VARIOUS MODES OF SELF EXPRESSION ARE OBSERVABLE IN RELATIONSHIP TO THE CENTER:

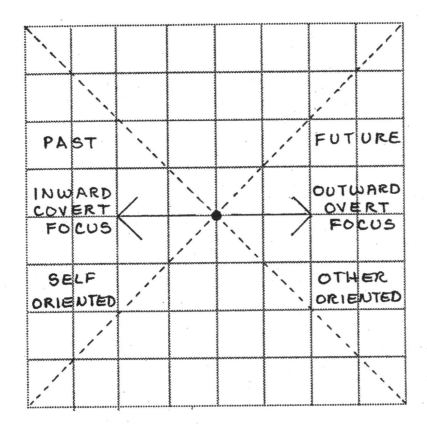

OUTWARD FOCUS: OVERT   Objects placed in the Outer Area represent an exterior focus. This Outer Area has also been said to represent the future.

INWARD FOCUS: COVERT   Objects placed in the Inner Area indicate a more reclusive, covert frame of mind. At times, objects placed here may also be symbolic of repressed feelings. This Inner Area has also been said to be an area representative of past experiences.   However in young children's drawings past and future references are rarely a pertinent issue.

INNER AREA: COVERT / OUTER AREA OVERT

In the following illustration two familiar "smiley faces" are placed on the drawing field. These faces represent other possible feelings related to the Inner and Outer Areas:

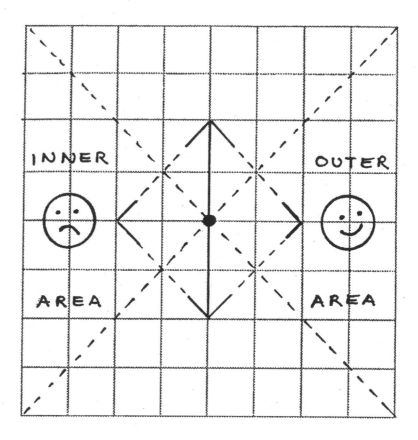

The smile on the Outer (public) Area and the frown on the Inner (personal) Area brings to mind the ambivalent feelings you may have when someone says, "Have a nice day".

The Inward Area is defined as covert (hidden) which implies a certain negativity is associated with this Area. While all objects placed in this Area do not necessarily indicate negativity; as noted on the prior page it also serves merely as a more private Area, because of the hidden implications it can be viewed as *predominately* negative. The actual objects drawn in this Area are the final determiners.

FACES OF FEELING:

These same smiley faces in the Higher and Lower Areas are representative of good and bad feelings:

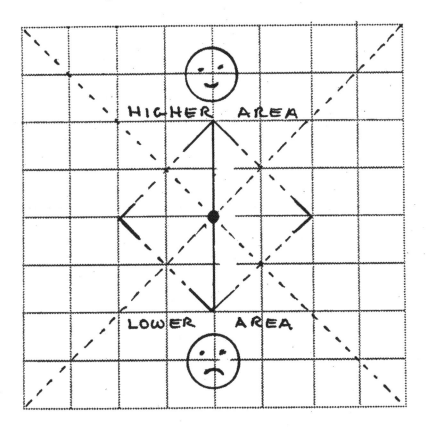

HIGHER AREA PLACEMENT: POSITIVE FEELINGS
LOWER AREA PLACEMENT: NEGATIVE FEELINGS

The child's ability to express feelings by the facial expressions they draw is unsurpassed even by the most talented of adult artists.   Even as the innocence of the child shines through in the execution of these simple drawings, a lot of emotional truth is revealed.

When the expression drawn reveals explicit feelings, emotional interpretation is easy, for although we have long since given up the practice, we have not lost the sensitivity required to understand the feelings implied. When there are no faces to "speak for themselves" placement of familiar objects on the drawing field provide clues to the emotional state of the artist.

THESE SMILEY FACES PLACED IN THE HIGHER AND LOWER AREAS ARE SYMBOLS OF " GOOD FEELINGS" AND " BAD FEELINGS".

Up-happy feelings are expressed by placing objects in the Higher Area. Down-unhappy feelings are expressed by Lower Area placement.

Children draw faces whenever and wherever they please. The placements shown here symbolize psychological associations with particular Areas of the drawing field and do not imply fixed placement.

Psychologically, Higher and Lower Area placements express good and bad feelings. Placement of objects in either of these Areas indicate either positive feelings (Higher Area) or negative feelings (Lower Area). Because a drawing is naturally physically oriented, the Higher and Lower Areas should be considered psychologically *predominate* positive or negative. allowing for natural physical orientation.

TWO AREAS SUGGESTING POSITIVE FEELINGS:

TWO AREAS SUGGESTING   NEGATIVE FEELINGS:

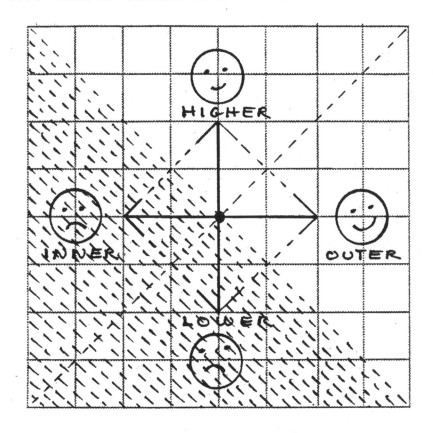

THE LIGHT AND DARK SIDE OF LIFE

This reference to the light and dark sides of the drawing field apply to the light and dark sides of life which is probably the definitive of all opposites. It is symbolic of the light and dark side of life. This concept is not beyond a child's psychological makeup, even though it would be an abstract theory they were unable to express verbally.

BALANCING OPPOSING FEELINGS

The drawing field provides special Areas that are reserved for the expression of both positive and negative feelings. The resulting drawing represents a visual ordering of these conflicting feelings. This ordering is a therapeutic experience, bringing with it a feeling of resolution. Young children draw as a form of self therapy, in which they are able to present, confront, and sometimes resolve things that bother them.

The early childhood drawing reveals a directing of positive and negative energies, an ordering of deep felt emotion - a balancing of opposing feelings. The drawing often acts at once as a cathartic and a healing.

Psychology as presented in this book relates to common everyday life experience. If you understand the feelings expressed by these smiley faces, you understand enough psychology to apply the principles given in this book.

THE DRAWING FIELD GRID

GUIDE TO LEVELS AND LOCATIONS

 **4**

CENTERED SPACE BOUNDARIES

THE CENTERED HOUSE AS ESTABLISHED BY THE CIRCLE   THE SQUARE AND THE DIAMOND:

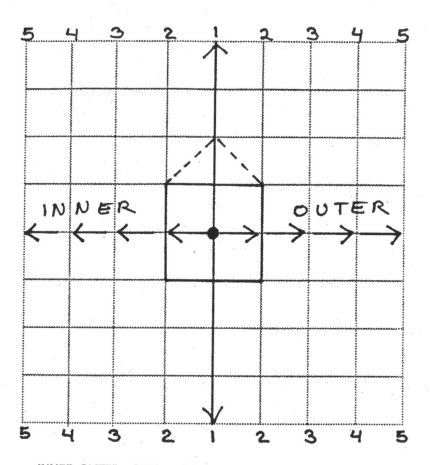

INNER-OUTER GRID LOCATIONS HORIZONTAL FOCUS

The Vertical Center Line establishes *CENTERED LOCATION ONE.* This Central Location Line divides the drawing field into Inner and Outer halves. The Outer half of the drawing field is divided by four additional vertical lines. As the Center is Location One, each successive line becomes Location Two, Location Three, Location Four and Location Five, which is actually the right edge of the drawing paper. Reading left to the Inner Area from the Center Vertical Line, is Location Two, Location Three, Location Four and Location Five, the left edge of the drawing paper.

THE HOUSE IS LOCATED VERTICALLY BETWEEN INNER AND OUTER LOCATIONS TWO.

HIGHER-LOWER GRID LEVELS

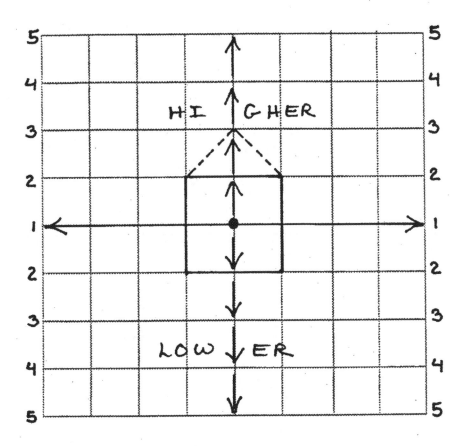

VERTICAL FOCUS:

The horizontal Center Line establishes *CENTERED LEVEL ONE.* This Central Location line divides the drawing field into Higher and Lower halves. Each of the Higher and Lower halves contain four additional lines which become Higher Level Two, Three, Four, and Five, which is the edge of the drawing paper. The Lower half becomes Levels Two, Three, Four, and Five. The house placed at the Center of the Grid is placed at Levels Three-H (Higher) and Two-L (Lower) and Locations Two-O (Outer) and Two-I (Inner).

THE HOUSE IS LOCATED HORIZONTALLY BETWEEN HIGHER LEVEL THREE AND LOWER LEVEL TWO.

EXPANDED CENTERED SPACE BOUNDARIES

A house conforming to the dimensions of the Center space as shown on the first Grid reflects the child's version of distance perspective. A house drawn that size is tiny compared to the size of the drawing field. Most house drawings are larger; closely conforming to an *expanded center space.*

THE ARROWS OF THE DIAMOND POINT TO LEVELS AND LOCATIONS THREE
DEFINING THE EXPANDED CENTER SPACE:

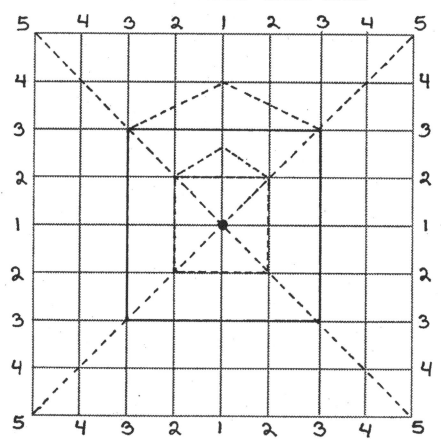

THE LARGER HOUSE SHOWN HERE OCCUPIES THE EXPANDED CENTER SPACE

BOUNDARIES DEFINED BY LEVELS AND LOCATIONS THREE WITH THE ROOF

EXTENDING TO HIGHER LEVEL FOUR.

PLACEMENT PATTERN

NUMBER ONE
(Central Focus)

 **5**

✳ ✳ ✳

Your child's drawings, reveal underlying placement patterns. Repeated particular uses of the drawing field suggests there is a subconscious understanding of, and compliance to, invisible divisions existing on the drawing paper.   In this section you will learn to recognize Placement Pattern Number One.

Although there are only three **primary** patterns: The Centered Main Theme; (Placement Pattern Number One): The Inner-Outer Horizontal focus; (Placement Pattern Number Two): and the Four Area Focus; (Placement Pattern Number Three) there are distinguishing variations on each of these.

This section is dedicated to Placement Pattern Number One. Illustrations are labeled as Number One A,   Number One-B, etc. These **secondary** patterns account for possible variations on the **primary** focus; the Centered Main Theme.

PRIMARY PLACEMENT PATTERN NUMBER ONE

THE CENTERED MAIN THEME OBJECT

Placement Pattern Number One , is recognizable by a centrally located object. A centered object, whether it be a house, animal, car, or a person sets the theme of the story told by the drawing.   In other words this object brings certain things to mind:

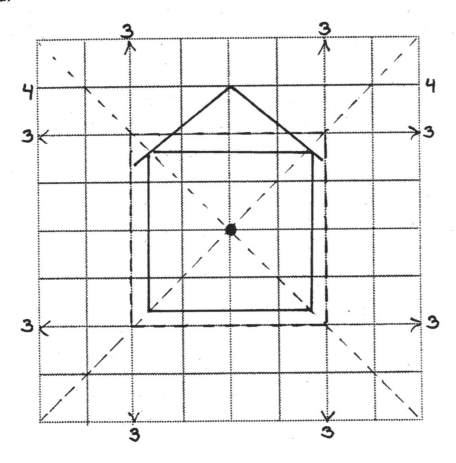

THE HOUSE AS A CENTRAL MAIN THEME

This example shows the house with the roof line extending beyond the Centered Space Boundaries into the Higher Area extending to Level four. While the Square part of the house is contained within the Center Space boundary lines this extended roof line lends an uplifting effect to the drawing that is observable to the viewer. This "up" appearance of the house reflects the "up" feelings in the artist.

Spaces between the grid lines, outside of the Centered Space boundary lines, allow for minor variation in placement while still conforming to the Center Space placement pattern. In various drawings any portion of the house may extend slightly beyond or lean into any one of the surrounding areas. These show inclinations toward the favored Area and should be interpreted keeping the psychological interpretation of that Area in mind.

In the next illustration the *entire* house is contained within the expanded Center Space boundaries. In this example of the child's version of distance perspective the house appears to be farther away than the large house.

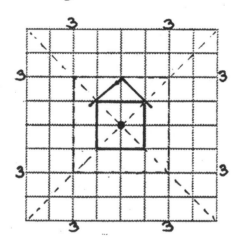

OUT FAR DISTANCE PERSPECTIVE

Note that this house also gives the impression of uplifted feelings even though it is completely contained within the Central Space boundaries. Although many more examples on interpreting Levels is upcoming, you will find that your own instinctive emotional response to be an accurate guide also.

SECONDARY PLACEMENT PATTERN NUMBER ONE A:

CENTERED MAIN THEME OBJECT/LANDSCAPE BACKGROUND

NOTE: LANDSCAPES ARE USED AS BACKGROUND IN THIS EXAMPLE, HOWEVER, LANDSCAPES MAY ALSO APPEAR IN ANY OF THE PRIMARY OR SECONDARY PLACEMENT PATTERNS FOLLOWING THE SAME PRINCIPLES.

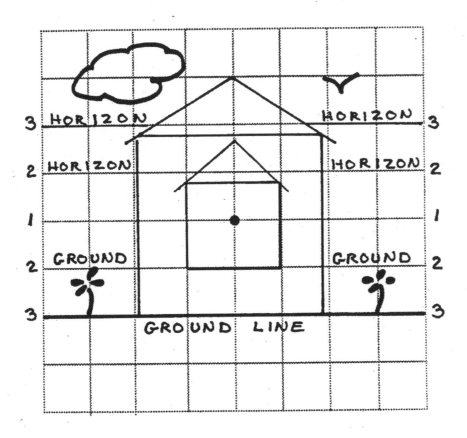

HORIZON AND GROUND LINES

This example of Placement Pattern Number One-A, shows horizon and ground lines as supporting background for the Centered object. Centered main theme drawings show close observation of the guide lines used in this example. The horizon and ground lines vary in keeping with smaller scale drawings within Higher and Lower Levels One through Three inclusive.

SECONDARY PLACEMENT PATTERN NUMBER ONE   B

MAINTAINING THE SECURE FEELINGS EXPRESSED BY CENTRAL PLACEMENT: GUARDED
AREAS - LOCATIONS 3-4

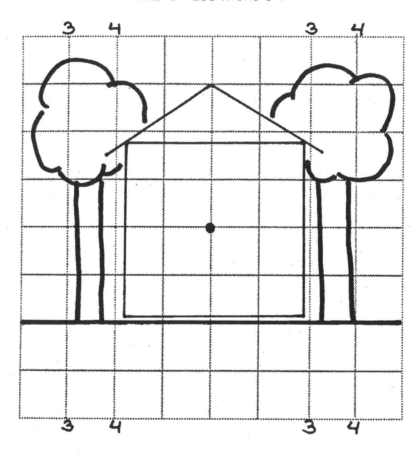

USE OF THESE "GUARD" LOCATIONS SHOULD ALWAYS CONSIDERED IN PRIMARY
PLACEMENT PATTERN NUMBER ONE.

In this example, trees are placed on either side of the house as
part of the landscape supporting the main theme. These trees
appear in the spaces between Locations 3 and 4 on both the
Inner and Outer focus'. Trees or other objects placed in these
spaces adjacent to the Centered object indicate a desire to
support a normal Centered feeling. When such objects are
placed in the Outer Area it indicates the artist has guarded
feelings toward someone or something. When placed in the
Inner Area shows a repression of disturbing feelings the artist
prefers not to recognize.

SECONDARY PLACEMENT PATTERN NUMBER ONE   C

THREE SECTION USE OF DRAWING FIELD:

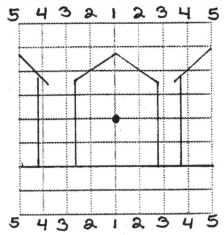

Additional houses or other large objects placed in Locations Four and Five flanking Central object. In some instances these objects will overlap into the guard spaces Three and Four. When this is so a certain guarded feeling is indicated.

SECONDARY PLACEMENT PATTERN NUMBER ONE D:

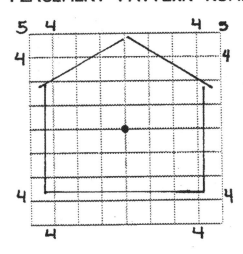

FULLY EXPANDED CENTER SPACE BOUNDARIES

Centered Main Theme object is drawn beyond normal Center Space Boundaries appearing between Levels and Locations Four and Five. Shows expansive feelings.

Drawing the Centered house appears to be an instinctive outlet for expressing feelings regarding the close associations with home and family.   Although drawings of the house are extremely common, children often *Center* other objects such as self portraits, animals, cars, etc.

You probably already have some of these drawings done by your own child. It is a good idea to begin saving them now. You may want to start a folder of "Centered Main Theme" drawings. Look for examples of each of the variations on Placement Pattern Number One shown here. Begin now to recognize these patterns and gain confidence in your abilities as you progress though the book. Later you can use the same drawings to further your understanding of the messages revealed in your child's drawings.

BASIC FORMS

NUMBER FOUR AND FIVE
(The Oval and the Rectangle)

 **6**

BASIC FORM NUMBER FOUR:

THE OVAL - THE SYMBOL OF SENSITIVITY

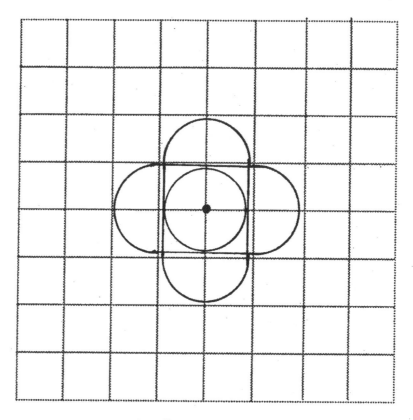

THE RELATIONSHIP OF THE CIRCLE AND THE OVAL

The circle, the self essence symbol is often drawn as an oval formation. The Oval is the fourth key formation but it is also a variation on the Circle indicating feelings of sensitivity or vulnerability. If you think of the oval shape of an egg you will understand the vulnerable feelings associated with this symbol.

The Circle and Oval as defined in the Pictographics symbol system represents sensitivities, however, circles and ovals used as wheels and faces etc., should be understood as representatives of the actual objects drawn.

BASIC FORM NUMBER FIVE:

THE RECTANGLE THE SYMBOL OF STRENGTH

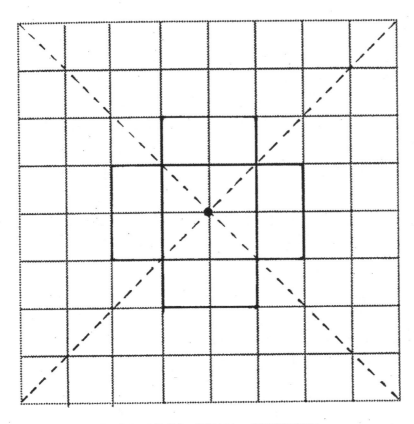

RECTANGLES EQUAL STRENGTH

The Rectangle is related to the Square as the Oval is related to the Circle. Whereas the Square symbolizes feelings of security, the Rectangle symbolizes feelings of self strength.

Curved forms are generally assumed to indicate feminine traits while angles are said to indicate masculinity. Pictographics recognizes curved Ovals and angled Rectangles as forms expressing the strengths and sensitivities of the artist regardless of gender.

Although Ovals and Circles are naturally curved forms - angles are often drawn suggesting curves:

CURVED LINES: ANGLED LINES:

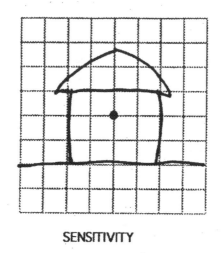   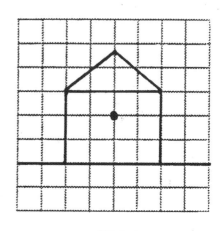

SENSITIVITY   STRENGTH

The house displaying mostly curved lines suggests a sensitive state of mind. The house displaying strictly angled lines suggests strong secure feelings. The Ideal drawing displays a balancing of combined angled and curved forms.

Curves and angles used in a drawing are secondary to actual object symbology and placement yet they establish feelings of strengths and sensitivities that might otherwise go unnoticed.

BASIC FORMS

(NUMBER SIX AND SEVEN)
(The Greek and Diagonal Crosses)

 7

BASIC FORMS NUMBER SIX AND SEVEN

THE GREEK AND DIAGONAL CROSSES

The final two forms of the symbol system are the familiar rays of the sun as shown on page 15:

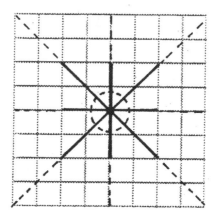

In this example these combined crosses are symbolic expressions of the child's natural energies.

Rare is the child's drawing that does not contain at least one of these symbols:

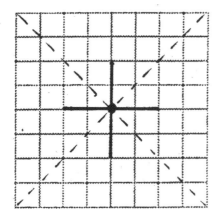

THE GREEK CROSS

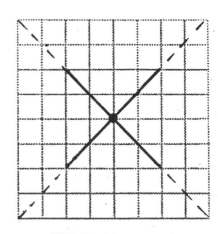

THE DIAGONAL CROSS

Very often these are drawn as a combine:

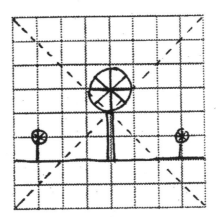

Children seem to be fascinated with these signs, decorating the sun, flowers, and tree tops as well as using them in normally expected places such as on windows, doors and car wheels.

These symbols are graphic expressions of energy (just like the sun's rays) when used in unexpected ways, such as forming flowers or trees.

When these forms appear in the Predominate Positive Areas they show happy exuberant feelings. When they appear in the Predominate Negative Areas they may indicate disturbing feelings. Keep in mind the child often draws to release and express pent up energies.

FREE FORM CURVES AND ANGLES

The *curve* and *angle* principle also applies to the Greek and Diagonal crosses. Any Line can be drawn. . .

AS ANGLES: OR CURVES:

With the addition of these "free form" lines any object can be implied in a simplified symbolic drawing.

The flowers in this drawing are examples of freely formed objects implying curves and angles:

THE PICTOGRAPHICS MANDALA:

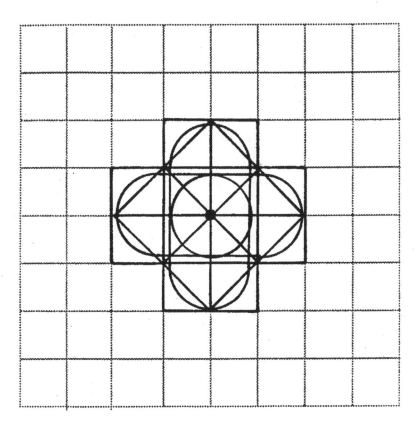

This mandala like design contains all seven basic forms of the Pictographics symbol system: the Circle; Square; Diamond; Oval; Rectangle; plus the Greek and Diagonal Crosses.

Can you locate and name all seven basic forms on the mandala? Find and trace the lines of the "sun" mandala as shown in the beginning of the book.

***

A mandala may appear to be nothing more than a decorative design; a formally organized work of art. However, the design contained within these symbolic forms is far greater than merely one of concentric geometrical forms surrounding a central focus.

This mandala conveys, in a pictographic way, the ability to order and organize the drawing paper into a logical field of physical and psychological orientation.

THE CHILD'S
GRAPHIC TOOLS

 **8**

THE SHAPE OF "THINGS"

THE SEVEN BASIC FORMS OF CHILDHOOD SYMBOLIC DRAWING:

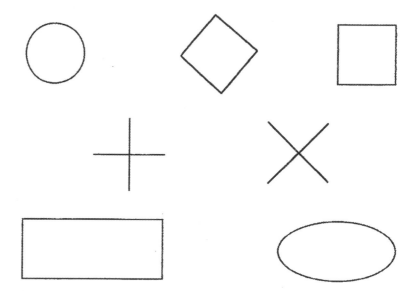

While these seven basic forms have special symbolic meanings within the Pictographics symbol system, they are also the building blocks of structure used by the child. A child's drawing itself is often referred to as "symbolic drawing" in that the objects created are symbols representing real objects. Any object can be symbolically implied in this way, by using wholes, segments, and combinations of these seven basic forms.

These geometrical forms are an integral part of life and learning. One of the child's first instructional toys is a square box with different shaped holes cut in the top. The "game" is to fit the round peg into the round hole, the square peg into the square hole, etc. Finding the right shape to fit in the right hole is a commonly used method of promoting and measuring both manual dexterity and intelligence.

These geometrical shapes are the building blocks of a structured world and it is only natural that these forms are also the building blocks of artistic expression. Rather than viewing the child's drawing as a crude effort to duplicate reality, train your eye to see these forms as the bare essentials of structure as the child does.

You can practice seeing in this manner by looking again at the world around you. The book you are now reading is rectangular in shape. The chair you are sitting on is most likely a square, with the legs and back following the rectangular lines. The room you are in is most likely square. Look around the room now and count the furnishings that follow the square and rectangular forms. How many circles and ovals do you see? Most of your surroundings follow the lines of the four basic forms: the square; rectangle; circle; and oval. The majority of objects are formed of the square and rectangular shapes and so these forms symbolize structure. The Lines provided by the diamond, the Greek cross, and the Diagonal cross, combined with the curved lines of the circle and oval provide all that is needed for the most ornately designed objects. The child's eye sees this, and their drawings are examples of their perception of simplicity; of seeing clearly, and should not be carelessly judged as inability to reproduce what they see. It is possible a child this age sees *the basic shape of things* more clearly at this stage of observation than he may ever see again.

THE CHILD'S SYMBOLIC DRAWING

On the following page there are examples of the child's symbolic drawing. These drawings are symbols in that they suggest the object they represent. These examples were done on the computer using the seven basic forms as wholes, segments, combinations and "free" forms.

SYMBOLIC DRAWINGS:

****

On a separate piece of paper try your hand at symbolic drawing. Use each of the seven "tools" as many times as you wish. Draw houses, people, cars, apple trees, swings, etc. Notice which "tools" or parts you are using or combining. You can have much fun doing this. If you just let go you will awaken many pleasant memories of your own childhood art. By expressing yourself through symbolic drawing again, you will also sharpen your "readers" eye.

PLACEMENT
PATTERN

NUMBER TWO
(Inner - Outer Focus)

 9

PRIMARY PLACEMENT PATTERN NUMBER TWO

PLANES-TRAINS-AND AUTOMOBILES-COMING IN AND GOING OUT

Levels Two and Three (on both Higher and Lower Areas) acting as Center ground and horizon lines as shown in Secondary Placement Pattern Number One-A, may also act as Inner-Outer action boundaries across the drawing field:

INNER/OUTER HORIZONTAL FOCUS:

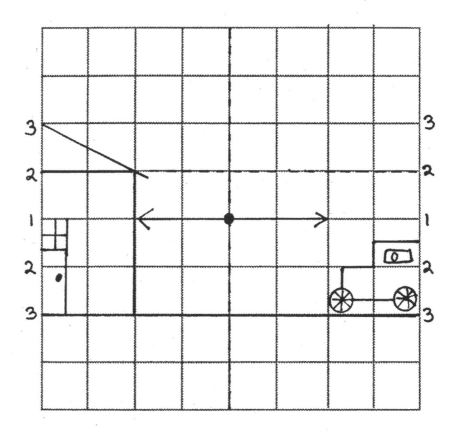

In keeping with the left to right writing practice - right is "out" and left is "in", **most** "moving" objects are shown entering the drawing field from the right facing left. This orientation suggests "others" are entering the artist's field of vision.

Objects placed in the Inner Area represent covert feelings regarding symbolic "Others" commonly placed in the Outer Area. In this pattern, the "Guard" spaces are not generally applicable.   The Vertical Center Balance line divides the drawing field into Inner and Outer halves:

SECONDARY PLACEMENT PATTERN TWO-A:

Objects penetrating the *Vertical Center Balance line* indicate an intrustion, showing an invasion of personal space:

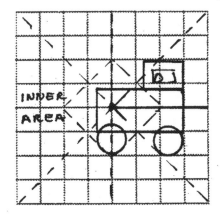

SECONDARY PLACEMENT PATTERN TWO-B:

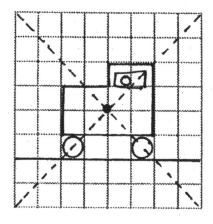

The   automobile or other moving vehicle occupying Center Space boundaries Three, reverts to a Centered Main Theme, as in Primary Placement Pattern Number One, however the focus implies inter-active relationships with attention focused on a specific outer influence. As with any Centered Main Theme drawing the Guard spaces should then be considered.

SECONDARY PLACEMENT PATTERN TWO-C:

UNUSUAL USE OF OUTER-INNER AREAS

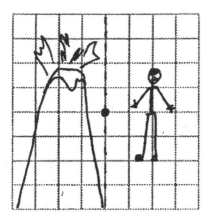

This illustration demonstrates one of the few instances when a self portrait is placed in the Outer Area.   In this instance the object(s) placed in the Inner area represent surpressed concerns.   The fire spouting volcano in this example is symbolic of pent up emotion on the verge of erupting. This example is a version of a child's actual drawing on page 97.

INTERPRETING

LEVELS

AND

LOCATIONS

❋ 10 ❋

SYMBOLS REPRESENTING SELF:

Very young children may not fully comprehend the separations of things and people apart from themselves. Instead they may view them as extensions of themselves. Houses and self portraits are often interchangeable symbols of self.

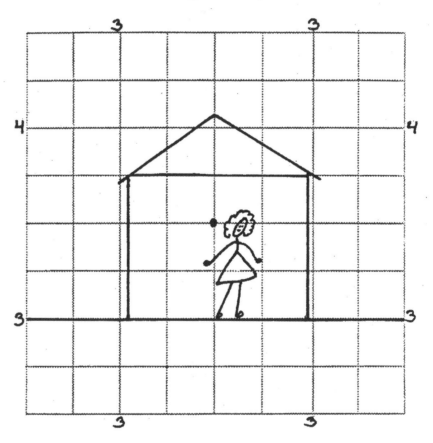

HOUSE AND SELF PORTRAIT-INTERCHANGEABLE SYMBOLS

Because of the close symbolic relationship between the house and the self portrait, the child may draw a house OR a self portrait to express his feelings. The following examples define feelings expressed by Level and Location placement of the house symbol.

EMOTIONAL HIGHS AND LOWS EXPRESSED BY HOUSE LEVEL PLACEMENT

The drawing field format, or shape of the paper drawn on, is as important a factor in determining Center balance as anything the child has drawn. Think of the drawing field as part of the picture. Balance and composition conform to this particular format.

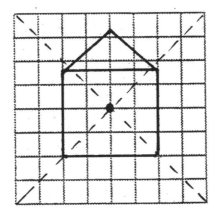

The Centered house is pleasingly "framed" by the edges of the drawing paper.

The two illustrations below show the house placed above the Horizontal Center Balance line (grounded on Level One) and below the Center Balance line (grounded on Level Five):

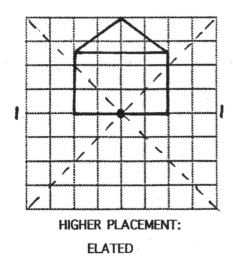

HIGHER PLACEMENT:

ELATED

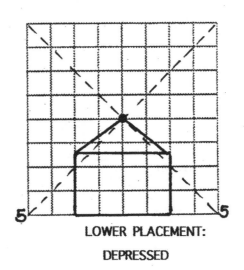

LOWER PLACEMENT:

DEPRESSED

It would not be possible to illustrate every conceivable Level placement a child might choose as the proportions of the house and the roof angle are both contributors to the overall balance and level implied (see page 32).   To determine High or Low Level placement compare the overall vertical dimensions of the house to the *Horizontal Center Balance Line*. If the majority of the object lies above this line, the house shows Higher placement.   If the majority falls below this center balance line, it indicates Lower placement.

On a scale of One (Center Balance Line to Level Five Higher, and One (Center Balance Line) to Level Five Lower, these Levels represent commonly experienced emotional *ups* and *downs*.

As most drawings are scaled to occupy the Center Space Boundary Lines; Locations and Levels Three, the remaining Level interpretations are simple ones. Placement in Higher and Lower Levels Four imply *good feelings* and *bad feelings*. Placement in Levels Five represent feelings of Elation and Depression.

These emotional fluctuations, are not meant to be taken as indications of serious clinical disorders, instead they represent the normal fluctuations which are a natural part of life.   If a child consistently drew disturbing pictures using only low level placement, the parent should seek professional help.

DETERMINING BALANCE:

At times, a child will use ground Level Five and yet the drawing composition reflects good balance as in the following illustration:

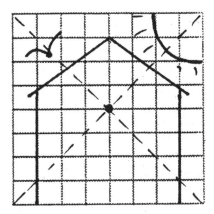

Keeping the shape of the drawing paper in mind, acting as a frame for the drawing, this lower level placement does not indicate depressed feelings as all objects are well balanced on the drawing field. A child who uses "all" the drawing space available, as in this example, has been accredited with an expansive nature.

Test your own emotional reactions as you compare these two illustrations. The illustration below shows imbalance in objects resulting in a depressed sensation in the viewer:

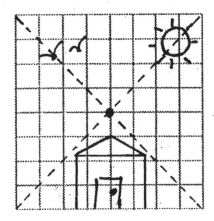

Note the "emptiness" of the Center Space, which has been left blank, disconnecting the Higher and Lower Areas of the drawing.

INNER-OUTER AREA *LOCATIONS*
HOUSE PLACEMENT INTERPRETATIONS

HOUSE CENTERED *LEANING* TO RIGHT OR LEFT:

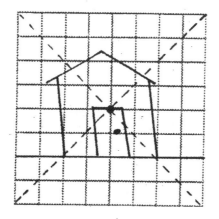

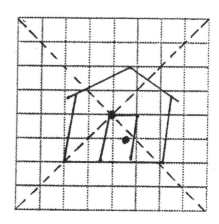

SUGGESTS INNER CONCERNS   SUGGESTS OUTER CONCERNS

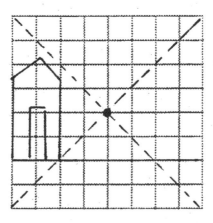

The house placed to the far left occupying Locations Three through Five shows feelings regarding self and home the artist prefers to keep to himself.

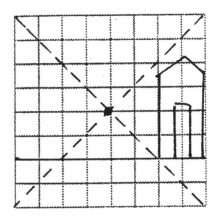

The house placed to the far *right* occupying Locations Three through Five of the drawing field normally indicates a desire to block others out. This rule applies only when the house represents the Main Theme of the drawing as in Placement Pattern(s) Number One.

If a house appears in this Outer Area in Placement Pattern(s) Number Two, which implies other orientation, it may be symbolic of a school, a store, or some else's house.

SYMBOLS OF INNER AND OUTER STRENGTHS:

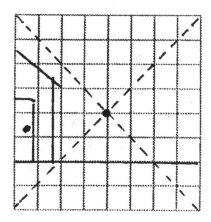 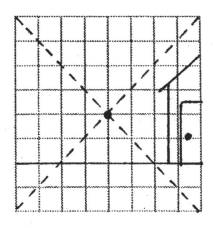

When only part of a house is drawn with strong rectangular lines this placement symbolizes Inner and Outer strengths. (See illustration on page 88). If the house is more curved, these symbols imply Inner and Outer weaknesses.

SELF PORTRAIT AND HOUSE DRAWING

SELF PORTRAIT *LOCATIONS* IN RELATION TO CENTERED HOUSE:

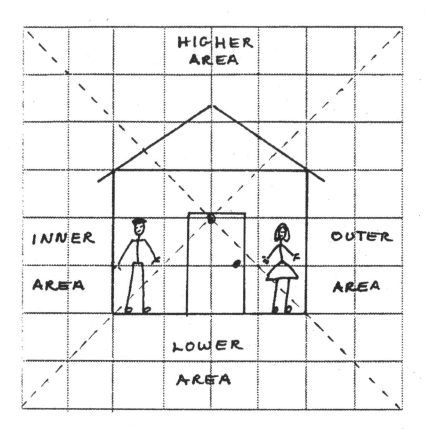

When the house represents the family and home environment the child often includes himself in the drawing. In this illustration the adjacent Inner-Outer Areas influence interpretation.

When the child places himself to the *right* of the house, contained within the Centered Space boundaries, he wishes to represent his home and family to the outer world.

Placement on the *left* within the Center Space boundaries indicates a desire to stand back and let others in his family take the lead.

CENTERED SELF PORTRAIT PLACEMENT

(PLACEMENT PATTERN NUMBER ONE)

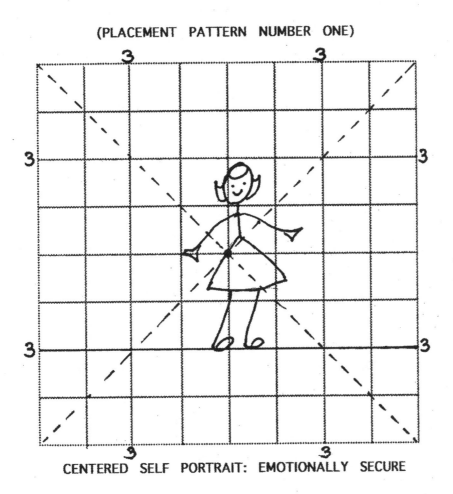

CENTERED SELF PORTRAIT: EMOTIONALLY SECURE

The Centered Self Portrait is another example of Placement Pattern Number One. As with the house drawing, landscapes and or guarded areas may or may not be used . Favoring (Leaning toward) the Inner or Outer Areas should be looked for as well as Level placements.

The following examples include the Centered house in the drawing, however, as these interpretations are made relative to the Center space the interpretations remain the same for self portraits appearing alone on the drawing field or when combined with other objects.

LOCATIONS OF SELF PORTRAIT

The following self portraits (moving outward horizontally from the Central focus of the drawing) occupy the spaces between Locations Three and Four in either the Inner or Outer Areas. As was noted on page 34 any symbolic object placed in these spaces indicate a guarded frame of mind:

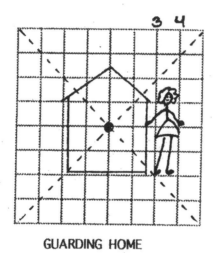

GUARDING HOME

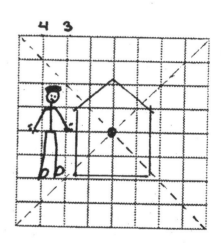

BLOCKING SELF DOUBT

Self portraits placed in the space between Locations four and five should be interpreted as follows:

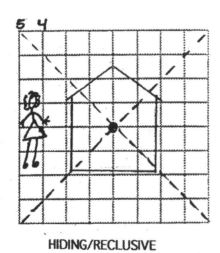

HIDING/RECLUSIVE

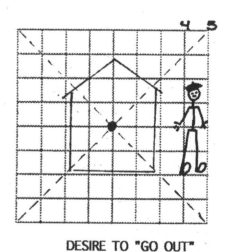

DESIRE TO "GO OUT"

LEVELS OF SELF PORTRAIT

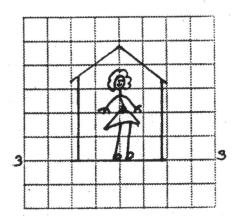

CENTERED SELF PORTRAIT

The following two illustrations show possible variations to this Centered self portrait expressed by varying degrees of Lower *Level* self placement:

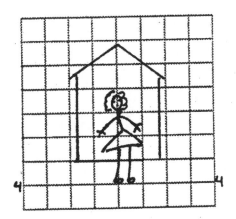

As has been noted, the Levels indicate varying degrees of feeling. The first self placement, grounded on Level four, indicates the child may feel insecure about his position of importance in the family structure. Grounding on Level Five could indicate a depressed feeling regarding the situation.

Elevated placement indicates elevated feelings. Placement on Higher Level Four corresponds with up-happy feelings:

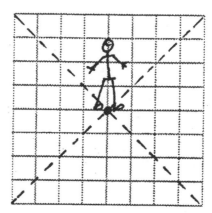

HIGHER LEVEL SELF PLACEMENT

The following illustration, showing the child on the roof, seems an unlikely placement. Children's imaginations are not to be contained at this age and to them anything is possible:

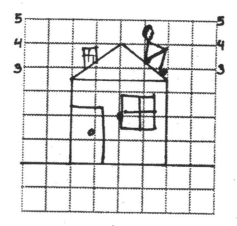

At times a self portrait will appear in the Higher Area. This high Level placement shows an elated, delighted frame of mind where a certain degree of playful fantasy is being employed.

PLACEMENT PATTERN TWO-C

GROUP PORTRAITS
INNER-OUTER FOCUS

SELF AND 'OTHER' *LOCATION* PLACEMENTS

In a group portrait (two or more people), the artist normally identifies with the Inner Area as the drawing field is shared with others who are placed in the Outer Area:

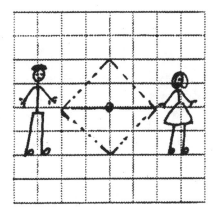

SELF   OTHER

"FRIENDS" BOTH WITHIN CENTER SPACE BOUNDARIES. *SELF* COMMONLY PLACED TO THE LEFT.

SELF/AUTHORIITY FIGURE(S). FIGURE CLOSEST TO CENTER IS ALSO EMOTIONALLY CLOSEST.

As is mostly the case in group portraits, the self portrait is placed to the left in the Inner Area. On the previous page, in the illustration showing authority figures, the "mother" is in the guarded position, with the "father" in the outer most spaces between Locations four and five. This Outer Area Location is most often used to place the person with the most authority as seen by the child.

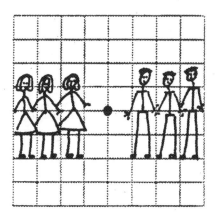

When many portraits appear in a drawing, look for close associations placed in the Inner Area and "outsiders" in the Outer Area. In a family portrait look for closest associations to be placed in the Inner Area or Centered Space.

Occasionally an uncommon placement occurs. While keeping the principles of Pictographics in mind also allow for this possibility. When there is a question in your mind regarding a placement ask your child how he feels about that certain person. One of the chief rewards for learning this system is the communication that results between you and your child.

SELF AND OTHER *LEVEL* PLACEMENT

ALWAYS LOOK TO PLACEMENT OF FEET TO DETERMINE LEVEL
COMPARISONS.

Level placements also reveal relationships between self and others. In this instance, the Higher and Lower Levels imply Levels of power between two people:

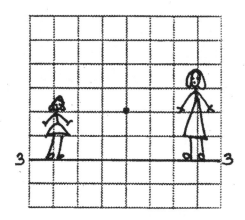

Both adult and child are "grounded" on Lower Level three implying equal status.

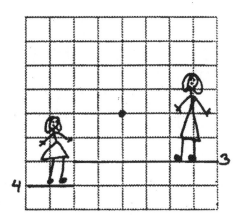

The child is grounded on Lower Level four while the adult is grounded on Level three. This placement indicates the child feels overpowered by the adult.

Even though the child is grounded on Lower Level three, which is the normal ground line of the Center Space, the adult is grounded on level 2 which is higher:

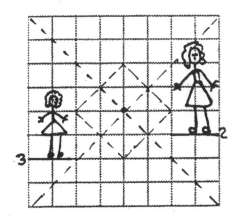

Depending on the story line told by the drawing, this elevated placement may indicate the person is held in high esteem by the artist.

A reversal of Level positions is shown in the following illustration as the child appears to feel he has the upper hand over the adult:

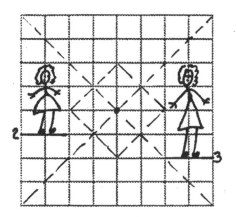

UNCOMMON PLACEMENTS

AREA PLACEMENT REVERSAL

Transient feelings of self importance may cause the artist to place himself in the Outer Area with the *other* person on a Lower Level of the Inner Area suggesting a negative attitude toward that person:

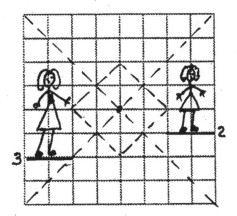

The following example emphasizes the possibility of either positive or negative feelings being expressed in either the *Predominate* Negative Inner or *Predominate* Positive Outer Areas. (*The predominating psychological allocations in these horizontal Areas are more subject to placement reversal than are the Higher and Lower Areas*):

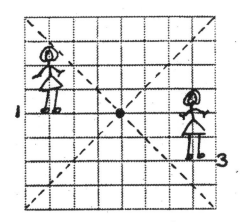

In this example the figure grounded on Lower Level four in the Predominate Positive Outer Area implies a negative impression of the person is held by the artist in relation to a Higher Level self placement.

Placement of another person in the Inner Area with feet grounded on the Center Balance Line (or Higher Level) shows a very close accepting relationship exists in the mind of the artist toward that person. Predominate Negative Areas are allocated as such because there is a tendency to keep negative feelings from public view. Many Positive feelings are also kept to oneself and this should be understood when interpreting a drawing.

As you can see by these *Area reversal* placements the Positive and Negative allocations are not absolute determiners but are designed to allow for flexibility of interpretation.

REMINDER: NEVER MAKE A NEGATIVE SUGGESTION TO THE CHILD REGARDING THE MEANING OF HIS DRAWING!

PLACEMENT
PATTERN

NUMBER THREE
(CENTER PERSPECTIVE - FOUR AREA FOCUS)

PRIMARY PLACEMENT PATTERN NUMBER THREE

CENTER PERSPECTIVE - FOUR AREA FOCUS

This third and final Placement Pattern emphasizes the need for viewing the drawing from a Centered Perspective when interpreting. This pattern *does not* draw the eye to the Center of the drawing with a large key object, as with Placement Pattern Number One, nor does it limit attention to horizontal object interaction as does Placement Pattern Number Two:

THE INTERPRETATION OF THIS FINAL PATTERN IS DEPENDENT UPON THE FULL UNDERSTANDING AND APPLICATION OF THE PRINCIPLES COMMON TO THE FIRST TWO PLACEMENT PATTERNS.

WHAT THIS DRAWING REVEALS

Looking from the Center horizontally, this illustration shows the house placed in the Inner Predominate Negative Area. This far left placement shows negative feelings regarding home life the artist prefers to keep to himself (see Locations illustration page 60). A portion of the house appearing in the "guarded" space between Locations three and four back up this impression.

A tree placed in the *Guarded* locations Three-Four in the Outer Area (see page 64) also reflects these reserved feelings toward the artists home life. This drawing reveals the un-centered feelings of the artist which is emphasized by the emptiness at the Center of the drawing.

The self portrait is placed on lower Level five indicating depressed feelings regarding the situation. (see page 65).

The central placement of the sun in the Higher Area is unusual as it is most commonly placed in the upper left or right corner of the drawing field. *When this placement is used it implies an effort is being made to center energies and emotions*. The ground line Level three placement of the house and tree is also a balancing sign.

The drawing also shows more curved (sensitive) lines than angles. Although this drawing does not appear to be primarily positive , keep in mind that *any* drawing your child does is positive in that it serves as an outlet for emotions that would otherwise go unexpressed.

SECONDARY PLACEMENT PATTERN NUMBER THREE - A
MISSING AREAS

At times, the message given by the child's symbolic drawing suggests itself by what appears to be left out. Placement Pattern Number Three-B is recognizable by any Area *obviously* missing from a drawing, disrupting the natural balance. In this example, the missing tree causes the drawing to look unfinished and lacks the natural balance that children naturally display in their drawings:

MISSING OUTER AREA

Loss of contact or interest with the exterior world is indicated by this particular Outer Area omission.

MISSING INNER AREA: MISSING HIGHER AREA:

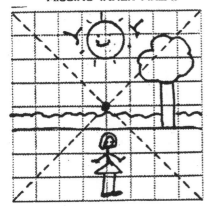   

Missing Inner Area does not reveal object of the concern which is still apparent by the placement of the remaining objects.

Missing Higher Area reflects feelings of hopelessness.

MISSING LOWER AREA:

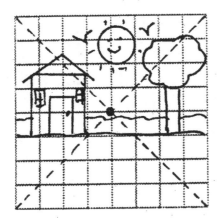

Many landscape drawings do not necessarily show much detail in the Lower Area. The ground is assumed to exist from the inferred ground line to the bottom of the drawing. When the over all balance of the drawing is lost due to *obvious* omission of the Lower Area, as it is in this example, it implies a repression of fearful feelings.

DIAGONAL   FOCUS   INTERPRETATION:

WHERE   LIGHT   AND   DARK   HALVES   MEET

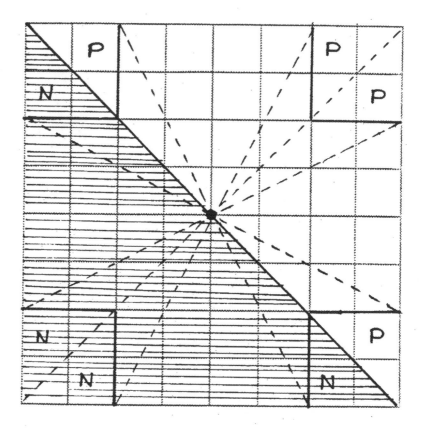

The light (predominate positive) and dark (predominate negative) halves of the drawing field share positive and negative assignments in the upper left and lower right corners of the grid. Objects appearing in these two corners, crossing the diagonal line, indicate mixed feelings.

Objects appearing in the upper right corner indicate double positive positioning. Objects placed in the lower left corner indicate double negative positioning.

LINE OF SPIRITUALITY

The upper right diagonal corner, intersected by the diagonal line, is the only double positive position on the drawing field. A spiritual quality accompanies the positive feelings associated with this position. The sun itself is an expression of the spirit and energy of life as experienced by the artist. This is the circle; symbolic of self essence, placed in the second most favorable position on the drawing field. The Center being the most favorable.

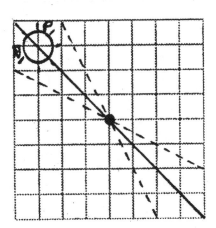 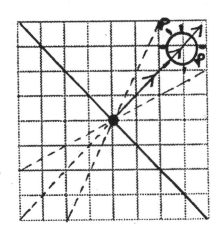

When the sun is placed in the upper left corner of the drawing field, it crosses over the division between the Predominate Positive and Predominate Negative halves of the drawing field. This placement shows mixed feelings, more positive or negative influence depending on which half of the drawing field is favored.

BALANCING POSITIVE AND NEGATIVE FEELINGS

The following picture shows a self portrait appearing in the lower left corner, intersected by the negative diagonal line, this places the self portrait in a double negative position as well as being grounded on level five, indicating depression:

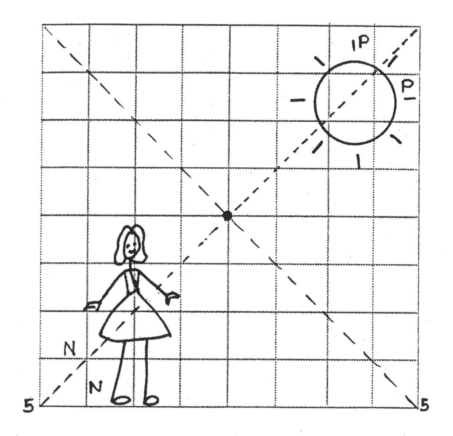

This placement is saved from ultimate negativity by the double positive placement of the sun. The double positive and double negative positioning reveals the therapeutic advantages of expressing conflicting feelings through drawings. Most drawings reveal attempts at balancing out positive and negative feelings.

SUMMARY

REVIEWING PLACEMENT PATTERNS
WITH ACTUAL DRAWINGS

CONSTRUCTING A GRID

 12

APPLYING PICTOGRAPHIC PRINCIPLES
TO ACTUAL DRAWINGS

The illustrations in this section are actual drawings done by a seven year old boy. Every drawing a child does shows a different aspect of his personality. You can "get to know" a child by looking at several of his drawings.

Because much of the subject matter and placement of a drawing is a subconscious experience it implies a state of *introspection* or a quieting of the mind. It isn't likely a child consciously decides to draw a picture about whatever is on his or her mind. Children instinctively find drawing a pleasurable emotional outlet.

The drawing reflects *subconscious* feelings regarding himself and his home and relationships. When discussing a drawing with your child do not expect conscious realization on his part as to why he placed certain objects where he did or what feelings that placement suggests. Avoid making him or her feel they are expected to explain their drawings.

REVIEW

PRIMARY PLACEMENT PATTERN NUMBER ONE:
CENTERED KEY OBJECT

Primary Placement Pattern Number One *always* features a large key form object such as a house, person, animal etc.   Very often the surrounding Areas are used as landscape background supporting the main central theme of the picture as shown in Secondary Placement Pattern One A.   Some drawings make use of the guard spaces as in Secondary Pattern One-B.

THE KEY TO DETERMINING THIS PATTERN IS THE APPEARANCE OF A CENTRAL MAIN THEME OBJECT.

When people appear in the surrounding Areas, their position is interpreted according to the rules common to all Level and Locations including Guard Locations 3-4.

The notations that appear with each of the following actual drawing examples should answer any questions you may still have regarding applying the Pictographics principles to your own child's drawings.

ACTUAL DRAWING ILLUSTRATION ONE

PRIMARY PLACEMENT PATTERN NUMBER ONE

CENTERED MAIN THEME:

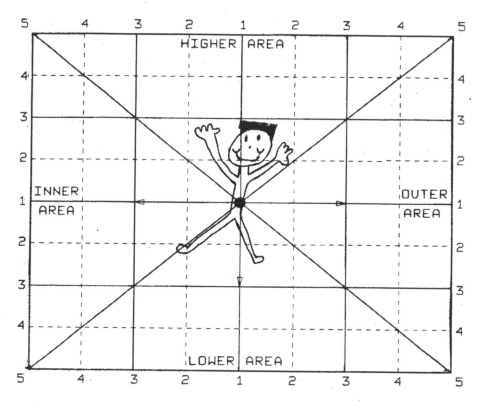

This placement pattern features a single object, in this instance the Centered self portrait. Clues to the emotional content of such a drawing are to be found in facial expressions when applicable and/or placement.

Self portraits, or other single objects are not always Centered. Placement of the object compared to Levels and Locations are indications of the emotional state of the artist regarding his *self picture*.

This particular drawing and placement shows a very up-beat, happy, energetic and well balanced little boy.

ACTUAL DRAWING ILLUSTRATION TWO

SECONDARY PLACEMENT PATTERN NUMBER ONE-A

LANDSCAPE/BACKGROUND:

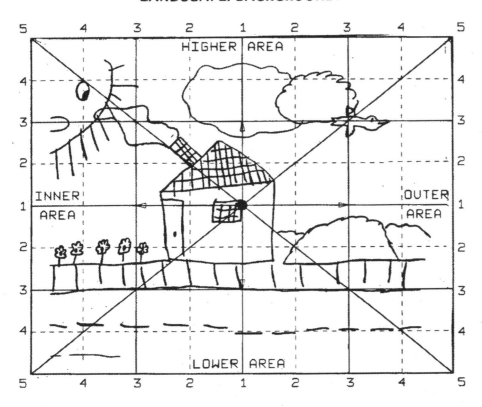

When you have reached this point in the book you should have a good grasp of what is meant by looking at your child's drawing from a new perspective. Instead of merely glancing at this drawing you probably have a good many ideas regarding the meanings of these placements. From this new perspective A drawing automatically captures your interest and tends to grasp your attention in ways it never has before.

While drawing this picture, the artist commented, "I want to write *'don't pollute'* in the smoke coming from the chimney". While he didn't do this the drawing itself tells the story if you look closely.

This house drawing is fairly well centered between Higher and Lower Levels three as the "sidewalk" doubles as a foundation of the house. This Center balance reflects a well balanced child who is inwardly concerned regarding pollution, which is symbolized by smoke coming from the chimney. The house placement favoring the left side of the Center space boundaries indicates an inward concern.

The alarmed expression on the *Sun's face* reflects this concern. The positive/negative placement implications of the sun in this drawing are clear; the fire in the house is symbolic of warmth and the smoke symbolizes ecological problems. The Inner Area of the drawing, in this instance, shows how the artist would like his world to be; full of flowers and clean air. It is interesting to note that the child personally identifies with many objects in the picture and each object reflects his feelings.

The Outer Area is not an Area of major concern. A bird flying to the right in an attempt to escape the smoke completes this drawing of a house. That pollution was on the artist's mind there is no doubt because he made that statement as he was drawing. Whether he felt this pollution to be a family problem would be an area of question. The parent might ask , "What pollution are you drawing about?" Be sure to follow the child's lead when you question. Do not make the drawing more psychologically implicit than the child feels it to be.

ACTUAL DRAWING ILLUSTRATION THREE

SECONDARY PLACEMENT PATTERN NUMBER ONE-B: GUARDED AREAS

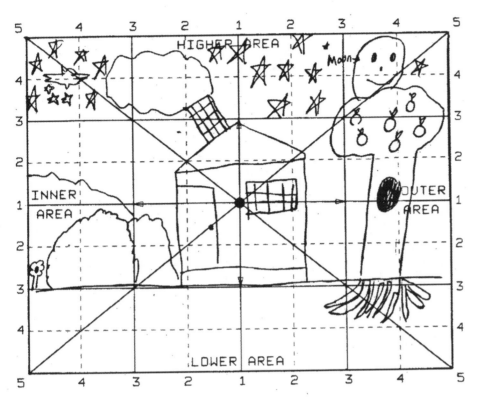

One of the most distinctive features of this drawing is the emphasis placed on the Higher Area of the drawing field from Level Three and up. This is a drawing showing the nighttime sky full of stars and the moon. Notice that the moon does not share in the rays of "energy" that are almost always drawn around the sun. This is a time of rest and the lack of activity around the moon stresses this feeling. The many stars and an unlikely bird (flying at nighttime) lend a feeling of fantasy that is often expressed in this Higher Area.

As a Centered house example the accent is on the night time sky and the Tree in the Outer "Guarding" position that one would expect in a scene such as this. The roots on the tree suggest added strength while the darkened Oval on the tree trunk speaks of a certain feeling of vulnerability.

ACTUAL DRAWING ILLUSTRATION FOUR

SECONDARY PLACEMENT PATTERN NUMBER ONE-C

THREE SECTIONS:

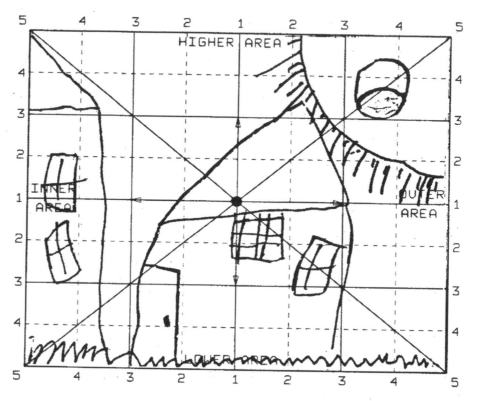

This drawing is an example of Secondary Placement Pattern Number One-C where the drawing field appears to be divided into thirds, with Center Space boundaries containing the Centered Main Theme object. Locations three through five on both the Inner and Outer Areas contain objects that support the Centered main theme.

The Centered house, grounded on Level Five, in this drawing suggests a depressed condition in the artist. In addition to the low Level grounding the house (which is drawn with many curved lines) appears to be slumping into the bottom of the picture. The roof of the house leans toward the enormous sun shown in the upper right corner of the drawing field. The size of this sun indicates a lot of sensitivity on the part of the artist. A smaller "sun/circle" appears drawn over the larger sun. This type of overlay has been said to be a sign of illness in the artist. The "spiritual" placement indicates a desire to rest in this drawing.

A taller, stronger looking house appears in the far left Inner Area extending into guard Locations three-four. This house symbolizes guarded feelings regarding present illness as well as the Inner strength that is the usual experience ofthe artist. This drawing was done late at night. While the drawing could reflect simple fatigue, it became known the following day the boy had a fever and a twenty-four hour bug.

When a drawing suggests depression, a simple question such as, "Do you feel tired?" may reveal the reason. When a single drawing such as this appears, there is no need for alarm, everyone experiences physical and mental highs and lows. If many drawings in a row cause you to feel the child is more depressed than usual you may want to talk to someone about it.

ACTUAL DRAWING ILLUSTRATION FIVE

SECONDARY PLACEMENT PATTERN NUMBER ONE-D

FULLY EXPANDED CENTER SPACE BOUNDARIES:

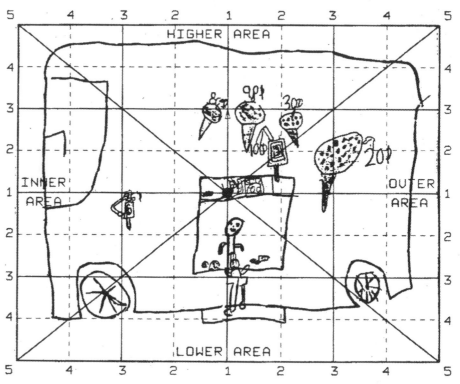

The normal Center Space boundaries, Levels & Locations Three, are expanded to Levels and Locations Four, in this drawing of an ice cream truck which closely resembles a border on the drawing field. Since there is much activity inside this "border" the eye is again drawn to the Center of the drawing field. The artist places himself on Lower Level Four with most of the Ice cream far above in the Higher Area (Center Balance Line One and above). Much of these "goodies" are out of reach because of the prices which are carefully noted. This drawing is an example of "Outer" influences and the resulting concerns. Because the Central focus is a "moving" object this drawing can also be classified as Secondary Placement Pattern Number Two-B.

REVIEW

PRIMARY PLACMENT PATTERN NUMBER TWO

INNER-OUTER FOCUS

This pattern is recognizable by suggested *interaction* between the Inner and Outer Areas. The subject of the drawing may be people, animals, or any object suggesting animation. Locations, Levels and in some instances, (review page 61) Guard space usage may apply.

Primary Placement Pattern Number Two also emphasizes the possibility of a reversal of positive or negative feelings expressed in the Predominate Negative or Predominate Positive Areas. Psychological allocations in these Areas are more subject to fluctuating placement than are the Higher and Lower Areas. To review this topic see Uncommon Placements page 71.

ACTUAL DRAWING ILLUSTRATION SIX

PRIMARY PLACEMENT PATTERN NUMBER TWO

INNER-OUTER FOCUS:

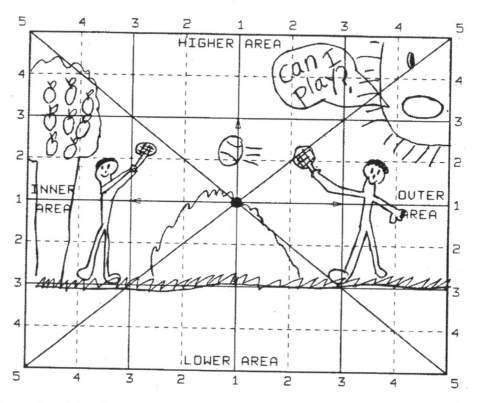

Although this illustration displays a Central object, the focus is one of Inner-Outer interaction. This horizontal focus drawing appears to be a study in an equal balancing of the Drawing field. The Center Space Boundaries surround a ball flying over bushes. The Self Portrait in the Inner Guard Space and the "other" placed in the Outer Guard space contain figures alike in size, height, and apparent abilities. The guard positions pertain to feelings of athletic prowess. The tree placed to the far right suggests an Inner strength is felt by the artist. He feels equal to any athletic challenge. The sun in the upper right corner suggests involvement of personal energies; the artists desire to play ball.

The curved forms in the Center Space Boundaries show feelings of sensitivity and desire for parental approval and attention. This is also indicated by the faces appearing to look toward the viewer of the drawing.

ACTUAL DRAWING ILLUSTRATION SEVEN

SECONDARY PLACEMENT PATTERN NUMBER TWO-A

VERTICAL CENTER DIVISION:

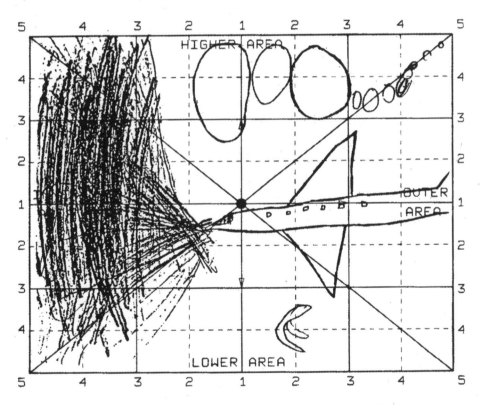

This drawing is an example of the child drawing as a means of releasing tension. It was done during the Gulf War crisis when television coverage was at its height. It shows the artist's personal reaction to what he was hearing from adults and seeing on the news.

An airplane enters the drawing field closely aligned with the Horizontal Center Balance line (Level One) dipping downward toward the Predominate Negative Lower Area as the nose of the plane extends into the Inner half of the drawing field. Gunfire begins in this Predominate Negative Area. From here, the artist first scribbled very dark black lines in the shape of the Inner Area boundaries. He then crossed these lines with curved scribbles. That the artist was experiencing a traumatic reaction to the current event is clearly revealed by these objects and placements. The airplane is a symbol of the threat with the *blackness* of the Inner Area representing personal fear and confusion.

Ovals, symbols of sensitivity, are shown entering the Higher Area on the upper right diagonal line beginning as tiny circles and expanding to become very large centered ovals. This upper right Diagonal Line is one symbolizing spirituality (see page 79). The circles appearing on this line indicate spiritual self association. As they become Ovals, they are symbolic of the vulnerable feelings regarding the safety of self and family. The centered Oval is symbolic of the artist placed between the two larger Ovals symbolic of his mom and dad; the other two members of his immediate family.

The smaller Oval crescent appearing in the Lower Predominate Negative Area is also representative of feelings of fear.

ACTUAL DRAWING ILLUSTRATION EIGHT

SECONDARY PLACEMENT PATTERN NUMBER TWO-B

CENTERED MAIN THEME:

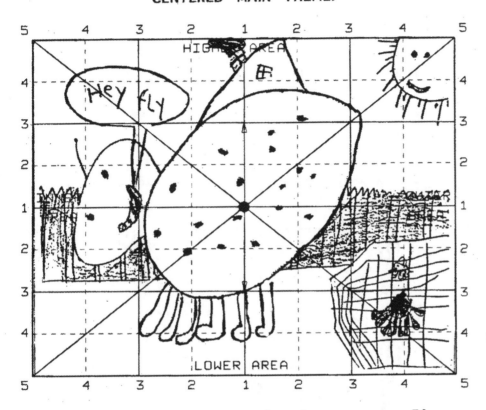

At first glance this appears to be the same as Placement Pattern Number One-A. The difference is an important aid to interpretation. This drawing shows an object entering the drawing field (facing left) suggesting relationships. The relationships of the spider, the fly and the Lady bug are the subject of this drawing. As the largest object, the artist identifies with the Lady Bug, who seems to have used this drawing to both express and overcome fears of the spider. The Lady Bug's Oval head is in the guarded space with a "whistling in the dark" type remark directly above.

A fence provides a background Center balance. The six legs in the Lower Area on Level four are well counter balanced with the main centered object. The "roof" of the house protruding from the Lady Bug's back extends into Higher Level Five shows a high level of confidence. The Oval forms of this drawing also show feelings of vulnerability. The Central balance, as well as the theme set by the drawing, shows this vulnerability is under control.

ACTUAL DRAWING ILLUSTRATION NINE

SECONDARY PLACEMENT PATTERN NUMBER TWO-B:

CENTERED MAIN THEME

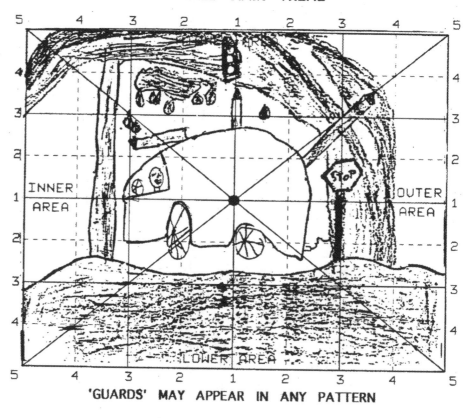

'GUARDS' MAY APPEAR IN ANY PATTERN

The Main object, a van, appears to have entered the drawing field and pulled to a centered stop. The van is bordered on each side, in the Guard spaces, by a stop sign in the Outer Area and a traffic pole in the Inner Area. The entire drawing is backed up by a rainbow overhead which does not reach the Inner Area suggesting repression of these feelings.

With more Ovals than Rectangals, this drawing shows sensitive feelings enclosed by protective guards. The strange objects emerging from the van appear to be smoking cigarettes. This drawing is symbolic of the artist's feelings of vulnerability to smokers in his family and his inability to remove himself from the situation. The driver of the van is a self portrait. He feels confident of his views as shown by the well Centered vehicle. The rain cloud overhead emphasizes the artist's disapproval.

ACTUAL DRAWING ILLUSTRATION TEN

SECONDARY PLACEMENT PATTERN NUMBER TWO-C

DRAWING FIELD HALVES:

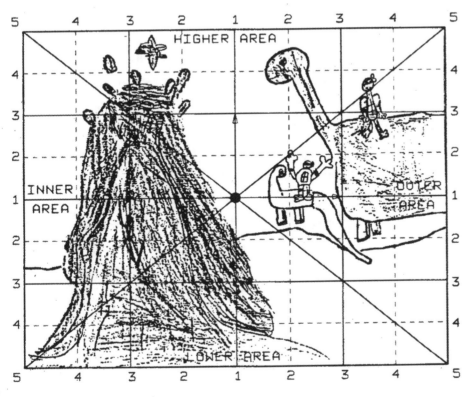

Several months ago the artist had a bad experience while at an exhibit of life size mechanical dinosaurs. He had a difficult time overcoming his natural fears about getting too close.

This drawing reflects his concerns, development and resolutions since that time.

The Outer Area shows these dreaded monsters teamed up with his favorite heroes, the Teenage Mutant Ninja Turtles. The rectangular shape of this dino indicates feelings of Outer strength, yet there are also many curves indicating feelings of vulnerability.

The objects in this Outer Area show a much higher ground Level in sharp contrast to the Level Five ground line of the volcano on the Inner Area. The Inner half of the drawing field reveals some reservations are still felt. This is indicated by an erupting volcano. The Oval lines of the volcano belie the strength suggested by this large somewhat rectangular form.

This drawing shows an Outer public version of the artist's feelings toward the Dinosaurs, compared to a more sheltered version which he keeps to himself.

It would be pleasant to believe the child's world was as carefree and happy as it often appears to be to the adult. In truth, they experience the very same feelings of security and insecurity the adult experiences. It may take some rethinking to accept that the cheerful little pictures they draw contain very real references to the problems they experience every day.

Note: Almost every drawing of a "moving" object shows it facing to the left of the drawing field. The artist who drew these pictures does alternate the directions taken by birds in the sky, however large key objects rarely vary from this rule.

REVIEW

PRIMARY PLACEMENT PATTERN NUMBER THREE
FOUR AREA FOCUS:

As the Placement Patterns are progressive, each dependent upon the one before, this final Placement Pattern best demonstrates the Whole picture and tests your ability to put to use the principles of Pictographics.

This placement pattern contains no Central point of interest and no particular focus point. It is this very omission that makes it comparable to Placement Pattern Number One where the focus is on the center of the drawing field. This pattern forces attention to the Center of the drawing in order to put it into perspective. Each Area is a vital component of the story told by the drawing.

This is perhaps the most creative and psychologically revealing pattern a child can use. It best demonstrates the scope and ordering of feeling the child is capable of.

ACTUAL DRAWING ILLUSTRATION ELEVEN

PRIMARY PLACEMENT PATTERN NUMBER THREE

CENTER PERSPECTIVE FOUR AREA FOCUS:

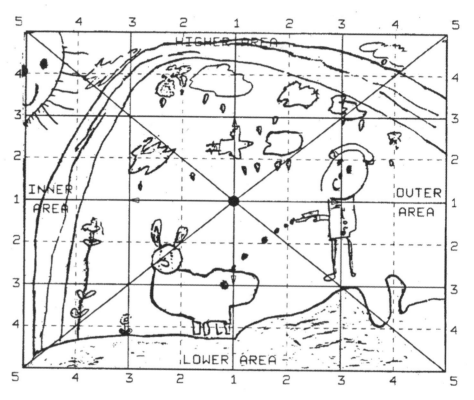

This drawing is primarily done with curved lines which emphasize the sensitive, vulnerable feeling expressed by the picture.

The Outer Area contains an authority figure placed partially in the Center Space boundaries and partially in the Guard space. This particular placement shows a guarded situation with a very close associate.

This illustration shows a self portrayal in the form of a lamb with a tearful face. These "human animals" are commonly drawn by children of this age. The lamb is grounded at the Fourth Level while the authority figure is placed on the Third

Level indicating a position of power. The artist apparently feels he has been "shot down" for some prank he pulled. It should be remembered that these pictures are drawn from the child's eye view and reflect how he sees situations that call for discipline.

A bird, (a favorite symbol that appears often in this child's drawings) appears in the Center Space facing outwardly showing a desire to leave. The Outer Area in this drawing is left blank indicating that this is a concern in the home rather than one concerned with outer conditions.

The rain clouds appear over the heads of both players in this scene, showing a mutual sadness. A second bird sits on a flower vine contained within the Inner guard space. This positive sign as well as the rainbow extending into the far left Inner Area suggests this experience is a brief one the artist is confident will soon pass.

The sun, appears in the upper left corner intersected by the diagonal positive/negative line. Placement of the sun on this line is always a sign that all is not well even though a smile may appear on the face.

DRAWING PAPER FORMATS

The most common size drawing is 8 1/2 by 11 with horizontal focus:

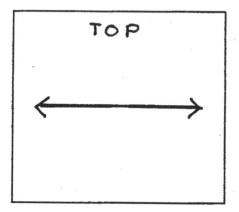

Occasionally, the 8 1/2 x 11 paper is turned so that the drawing has a vertical focus:

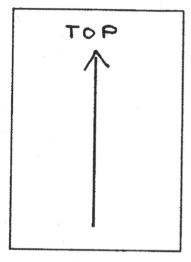

The Pictographics grid adapts to any size or shape of paper as long as the top and the bottom of the picture are noted.

ACTUAL DRAWING ILLUSTRATION TWELVE

VERTICAL USE OF PAPER:

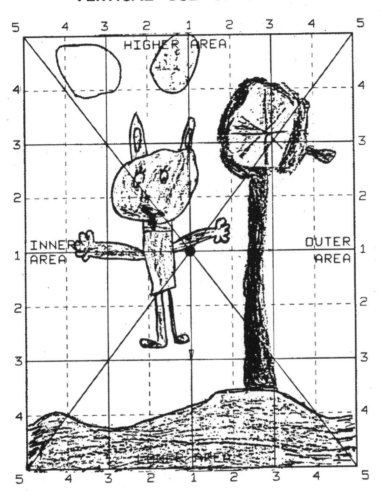

Again the artist portrays himself as half human half animal. This "self portrait" shares the Center space (Levels and Locations Three) with a tree which is a symbol of self strength. The tree top is a combination of the Greek and the Diagonal crosses (expressions of the artist's energy).

This tree, is firmly grounded unlike the self portrait. This half-boy half-rabbit finds himself in a perplexing predicament, shown by the facial expression, as he notes his ungrounded position. The ground line at the lowest point is Level Four under the rabbits feet positioned slightly above Level Three. His arms located on the Horizontal Center Balance Line appear to be attempting to balance himself.

This drawing seems to be about a child who must control his enthusiasm and energies and to so leaves him feeling ungrounded.

* * *

As you take the time to study your child's drawings you will find yourself becoming more attuned to the psychological language of the drawing. Some of your observations will be beyond the child's understanding. Refrain from an obvious psychological discussion. Keep this a fun experience the child will look forward to.

CONSTRUCTING A GRID

In this section, while folding the drawing paper to establish Pictographic grid lines, you may at the same time, test your knowledge of the Areas, Levels and Locations.

The grid guide lines can be transfered to any size drawing. It is best to use a plain piece of paper for practice. You can also practice on different sizes of paper.

CREATE A GRID BY FOLDING THE PAPER

Create a grid on a blank piece of paper as you go. These folds will create an outline of the grid. Using a plain 8 1/2 x 11 sheet of paper, make folds according to the following directions.

First, fold the paper from corner to corner diagonally, as shown below. Locate and mark the exact Center of the drawing field. This initial fold creates the Diagonal boundary lines of the four Areas:

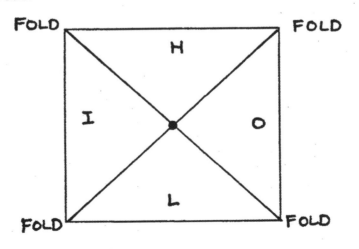

Identify each Area with one of the following; H for Higher, L for Lower, I for Inner and O for Outer. Mark these in with a pencil.

Next fold the paper exactly in half on both vertical and horizontal lines. These folds divide the drawing field into Higher and Lower halves and Inner Outer Halves:

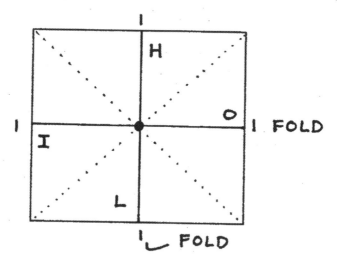

Now, fold each Higher and Lower *section* in half horizontally:

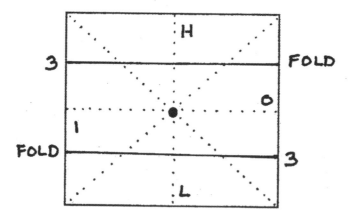

These folds define the Horizon and Ground lines (Levels three) when used as a Landscape background as well as establishing the Inner-Outer focus *action boundaries* of Placement Pattern Number Two.

Next, fold the Inner and Outer Area *sections* exactly in half:

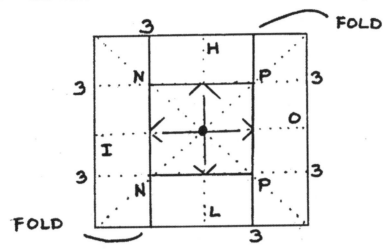

This fold defines the Center Space boundaries. Draw in these boundary lines (Levels and Locations three).

Sketch in the Diamond arrows pointing to each Area, stopping at the Center Space boundaries.

The main lines of the grid establishing the Center Space boundaries and the Areas are now established. To complete Levels and Locations, **sketch*** lines midway between each of these main folds:

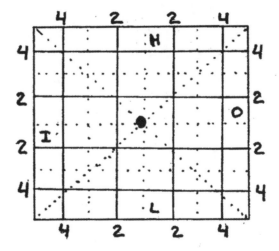

*It is easier to sketch these additional grid lines than to fold the paper.

Mark all Locations beginning with Level One at the Vertical Center Balance Line. Mark all Levels beginning with Level One at the Horizontal Center Balance Line.

Check your completed grid against this example:

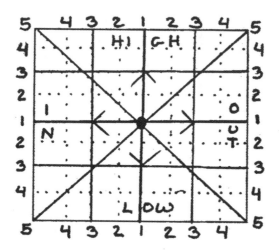

If you prefer, as an alternative to folding the drawing, you can make up an overlay using an envelope type transparent paper holder using a very thin graphic arts tape, which comes in many colors, to mark the grid lines. Different colors can be used to define various key divisions (as shown here) on the overlay making them easy to see. As the most common drawing paper is 8 1/2 x 11, you may want to use this size transparent envelope. The drawing can be slipped into this envelope confining it within the grid for accurate placement interpretation.

INTERPRETING   TIPS:

The following outline will serve as a guide as you begin to apply Pictographic's placement principles to your own child's drawings:

DECIDE WHICH PLACEMENT PATTERN DOMINATES THE DRAWING. LOOK FOR THE MOST DISTINCTIVE FOCUS. THIS WILL HELP YOU CHOOSE THE BEST AND MOST ACCURATE METHOD OF ADDING TO YOUR UNDERSTANDING OF THE DRAWING.

DOES THE DRAWING CONTAIN MORE CURVED OR ANGLED FORMS? DO THE STRENGTHS AND SENSITIVITIES INDICATED BY THESE BALANCE OUT?

LOOK FOR POSITIVE AND NEGATIVE FEELINGS REVEALED BY LEVELS, LOCATIONS AND AREA PLACEMENT.

CHECK FOR POSITIVE AND NEGATIVE DIAGONAL LINE CORNER PLACEMENT.

ARE THERE ANY SIGNS OF GUARDED FEELINGS? WHAT DOES THE ARTIST APPEAR TO BE GUARDING AGAINST?

Always look for signs of balance and counter balance. After all the child often draws the picture as a way of resolving conflicting feelings.

Drawing turns the creative mind to expose its workings. Drawing discloses the heart of visual thought, coalesces spirit and perception, conjures imagination; drawing is an act of meditation.

-Edward Hill
The Language of Drawing, 1966

AFTERWORD

The ability to interpret the feelings implied by object placement adds emotional depth to the story told by the drawing. While this is so, do not underestimate the importance of the story the child is reflecting upon. The stage of this one scene emotional drama is set by the props and the characters. The "star" of the show is always the artist, even though he or she may not physically appear in the drawing.

Looking at a child's drawing from your new perspective you will no doubt view it more clearly than you did before, because now you will find that you are "seeing" and not merely glancing at the drawing . With practice, you will automatically notice various Area and Level and Location placements and be immediately aware of their emotional implications. Even when this ability becomes second nature to you, do not overlook the story the child is telling. Children love it when you pay special interest to their drawings. You should now be able to discuss the drawing with the sincere interest the child hopes for. Your remarks should be in keeping with the dignity and privacy of the child in mind. Your insights into varying emotional inclinations of the artist should be treated as adult material.

After reading and using the principles provided in this book, your child's drawings will not only become a source of greater pleasure to you, some will take their rightful place as a special "picture album" record of their childhood. The very least you will gain from this book is a new appreciation of these drawings. At most, you will gain a new appreciation of the emotions you have in common with your child.

There are those who might argue that varying degrees of development of muscular control, intelligence and artistic ability represent the main ingredients in an example of individual artistic effort. While these obviously play a part from an aesthetic point of view they do not limit the degree of self expression possible. Eventually a lack of artistic ability may cause a child to stop drawing altogether. When this happens, a valuable source of emotional expression is lost forever. This doesn't have to be. . .

ADULT SYMBOLIC DRAWING - SELF ACTUALIZATION

The two following mandalas were drawn by young adults, male and female, when asked to draw how energy *felt* to them:

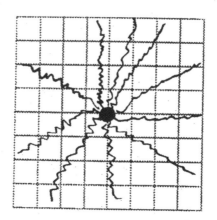 

Although the male and female personalities are not difficult to guess - The first drawing was done by a 23 year old man - the second by a 19 year old woman - their drawings share in the concept of lines symbolic of energy radiating out from a Central nucleus. These choices reflect an awareness of the Central focus common to Pictographics, which indicates the adult has retained subconscious awareness of the orientations common to symbolic childhood drawing.

The therapeutic benefits of childhood drawing can be re-experienced by you as an adult. There is much talk about becoming aware of the "child within" these days, and while I might suggest you focus on this child within as you draw, the purpose of doing these spontaneous drawings is not to reflect on your childhood but to focus on the problems you have today. As drawing is a form of meditation, you will find it relaxing and even fun to do if you just "let yourself go".   Do not be concerned about your artistic abilities while you do this for these aspects have nothing to do with the success of your Pictographics spontaneous drawing.

As you draw, it is possible you may not consciously focus on anything at all and just allow your drawing to *happen* which is most likely the way the child consciously experiences drawing.

The most productive method, however, is to draw with a specific problem in mind.   Draw a "scene" describing the situation. If there are other people involved, sketch them in. Place everyone and everything quickly, remember artistic ability doesn't count.

You may feel that since you are aware of the implied emotional implications of the Areas, Levels, and Locations you will be influenced by this knowledge to deliberately place things where they will reflect you best. You will be surprised to find this is not the case. Allow your drawing hand to be guided where it wants to go and to draw what it wants to draw. When you feel the drawing is complete, write a title beneath it that best sums up your story.

The moment of truth comes when you apply the grid lines to your drawing. It is not easy to fool your subconscious mind. Your true feelings regarding the "situation" are clearly revealed as you compare your placements with the interpretations given in this book.

You may want to write a new title for your drawing based on your insights. These insights come from your subconscious mind where your true feelings are often hidden from your conscious awareness. You may also want to end your symbolic drawing session with a message *to* your subconscious mind. Sketch a drawing that reflects your conscious wishes and desires. *This drawing is a conscious projection of how you want things to be.* In doing this, you are engraving positive images on your subconscious mind. You are Centering your mind on your choice and not merely allowing conflicting feelings to lead you where they may.

People who have tried positive visualization techniques as a means of self actualization may find this method more effective as they can actually *see* the image they wish to hold in their mind. Post *this* picture on your refrigerator door (or in a more private place if the message is personally yours) and you will reinforce your positive mental image many times a day.

Symbolic drawing *from* the subconscious mind should also be done frequently; at least once a week or any time you are particularly troubled. By doing this, you will keep your mind cleared of subconscious resistance to the new ways you have chosen to experience life.

As you begin to save your child's drawings as a record of these "special years" you may also want to save your own symbolic drawings, noting your progress as more positive images naturally flow from your subconscious as your draw.

* * *